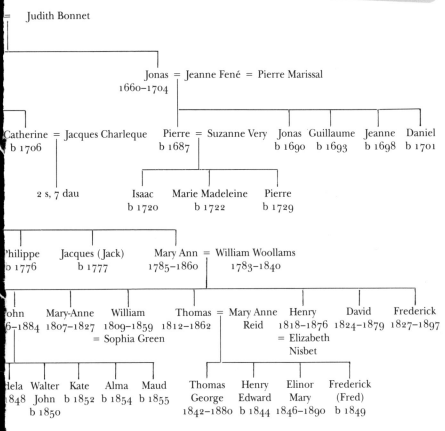

= Judith Bonnet

Jonas = Jeanne Fené = Pierre Marissal
1660–1704

Catherine = Jacques Charleque   Pierre = Suzanne Very   Jonas   Guillaume   Jeanne   Daniel
b 1706   b 1687   b 1690   b 1693   b 1698   b 1701

2 s, 7 dau   Isaac   Marie Madeleine   Pierre
                    b 1720   b 1722   b 1729

Philippe   Jacques (Jack)   Mary Ann = William Woollams
b 1776   b 1777   1785–1860   1783–1840

John   Mary-Anne   William   Thomas = Mary Anne   Henry   David   Frederick
6–1884   1807–1827   1809–1859   1812–1862   Reid   1818–1876   1824–1879   1827–1897
                         = Sophia Green   = Elizabeth
                                                     Nisbet

...dela   Walter   Kate   Alma   Maud   Thomas   Henry   Elinor   Frederick
1848   John   b 1852   b 1854   b 1855   George   Edward   Mary   (Fred)
           b 1850   1842–1880   b 1844   1846–1890   b 1849

indicates
adoption

THE
AUMONIERS

For Regina
with love
Ann

THE
AUMONIERS

CRAFTSMEN & ARTISTS

a family memoir
by
Ann McGill

HIGHLANDS BOOKS
NEW CITY, N.Y.

Published by Highlands Books
41 Third Street, New City, N.Y. 10956
Copyright © Ann McGill, 1998

The illustrations 'Hall seat in English oak,' from *The International Studio,* 1900, vol. IX, and 'The keystones at York House,' from *Modern Architectural Sculpture* by William Aumonier, are reprinted with the kind permission of Avery Architectural and Fine Arts Library, Columbia University in the City of New York.

Excerpts from the letters of Julia Aumonier and William Aumonier to Pierre Aumonier are printed with the kind permission of Annette Hilton.

Excerpts from the diary of Whitworth Aumonier are printed with the kind permission of Elisabeth Hopkins.

The ornament on the title page is from a sketch of a piece of jewelry by Henry Aumonier.

Design and production: Martyn Hitchcock

Manufactured in the United States of America

ISBN 0-9666710-0-7

for
Alexandra and Benjamin

‹ ❋ ›

Contents

‹ ❋ ›

Illustrations

‹ ❊ ›

Preface

I have written this book as I want to record the history of the Aumônier family from 1685, when Pierre and Jonas Aumônier fled from France to England, to the present time. I have attempted to document the family genealogy, the artistic achievements and heritage, and the strong family ties that existed over several generations. As this book covers over three hundred years I have included some brief descriptions of social conditions and history to place the reader in context with the time under discussion. I have also described several pieces of art in some detail, but this is not an art book. It is a family history and it is also a story. I have woven together the lives of people who lived three hundred years ago with their descendants in subsequent generations.

The material is drawn from family letters and papers, articles and reviews, and the publications of the Huguenot Society of London.

There are several variations of the spelling of Aumônier in the old records, including Au Mosnier, Ommonier, Amanier, Omonier, and Homonier. Many of the record-keepers in the late seventeenth and early eighteenth century were unfamiliar with the French language, and a name was frequently spelled as it sounded.

English spelling was used for most of the entries in the court books of the Weavers Company.

The earliest reference I found to the name Aumô-nier was in *Huguenot Pedigrees* by Charles Edmunds Lart:

Louis Buor, éc., sgr. de La Gerbaudière, received an act of homage from Etienne Sereneron, éc., sgr. de Boislambert, 20 June 1480. He married Dlle. Marie de Granges, daughter of Jean de Granges, éc., sgr. de Puychenin and of Dlle. Mau-ricette Aumosnier.

I have been unable, however, to establish a direct link between Mauricette Aumosnier and Pierre Aumônier, who is one of the first people in our story.

My thanks go to Elisabeth Hopkins, Annette Hilton and Malcolm Ford for providing family papers, photo-graphs, and letters; and to Mary Allison, Martyn Hitch-cock, Jennifer Shapiro and my family for their advice, encouragement and assistance.

THE
AUMONIERS

⟨ ✻ ⟩

Prologue

THE AUMÔNIERS are of Huguenot descent. The origin of the term 'Huguenot' is disputed, but by the middle of the sixteenth century the term was being used to describe French Protestants. There are many explanations of the term: one links it to King Huguet's gate at Tours, another to the medieval French king Hugues Capet. In the seventeenth century, the province of Poitou in western France at the northern end of the Bay of Biscay was a stronghold of the Huguenots in their struggle against the Pope.

In 1598 Henry IV of France signed the Edict of Nantes. This had a great effect on the lives of the Huguenots and they attained a freedom they had not had in the past. They were granted the right of worship in most towns, and the royal treasury made an annual contribution towards the salaries of Huguenot pastors (there were about one hundred Huguenot churches in Poitou and neighbouring Saintonge and seven hundred and fifty in all of France). A Protestant chamber was established in the Parlement of Paris, joint chambers in other local parlements, and the Huguenots were given territorial guarantees that allowed them to occupy, at the expense of the King, one hundred fortified towns.

3

Henry IV died in 1610, and his young son, Louis XIII, became king. He was nine years old and his stepmother, Marie de' Medici, was proclaimed regent. She soon became a pawn in the hands of Concini, an adventurer who assumed a condescending guardianship over the boy King. Louis tired of Concini and in 1617 ordered his arrest. Concini resisted, but died in the ensuing scuffle. Charles d'Albert de Luynes replaced Concini as advisor to the King. The princes and nobles did not like de Luynes any more than they had liked Concini, and they were convinced that their power was in jeopardy. The Huguenots were also apprehensive and determined not to lose their religious and political privileges. In 1624 Cardinal Richelieu seized the helm and for the next eighteen years was the power behind the throne. He was determined to destroy the Huguenots and diminish the power of the nobles.

La Rochelle had long been the capital of the Huguenots, and in 1627, when England declared war on France and British forces landed on the Ile de Ré, an island off the coast opposite La Rochelle, the Huguenots sided with the British. Richelieu prepared for war against La Rochelle. The city was well protected. It was surrounded by strong walls and had two natural harbours formed by the Ile d'Oleron and the Ile de Ré, and it could withstand a siege. Richelieu decided to cut off all supply routes, and it was not long before there was a severe shortage of food. The Rochellois held out for fourteen months, but on 28 October 1628 Louis XIII and Cardinal Richelieu rode victorious into the starved and besieged city. Fifteen thousand people had died of famine during the siege and many of the dead still lay unburied in the streets. There were no severe punishments following the siege, however, and the Huguenots continued to enjoy freedom of worship.

Cardinal Richelieu died in 1642, and Louis XIII died the following year leaving his five-year-old son Louis XIV to succeed him. Once again there was a child king on the French throne; Cardinal Mazarin, Richelieu's successor, controlled the government and continued to do so until his death in 1661, even though Louis came of age in 1651. Louis XIV was known as "The Most Christian King," but he hated the Huguenots. When he assumed control of the government, he issued a manifest requiring all citizens to assume his religion, that is, Roman Catholicism. He further expressed his hostility by declaring that the Huguenots were not good citizens. They were in reality, however, not only loyal and prudent citizens but quiet, hardworking, and thrifty people who wanted to live in peace.

On 18 October 1685 Louis XIV signed an ordinance revoking the Edict of Nantes. He had convinced himself that the Edict affected very few people and that it was injurious to the realm. He then ordered all Huguenot ministers to leave France and threatened to execute those who disobeyed him. Their congregations were expected to convert to Catholicism. This was too much for the Huguenots, who had fought before for their religious freedom and were already ill-treated and repressed. Thus began a great exodus. Well-educated bourgeois, prosperous merchants, and skilled artisans and craftsmen were among those who left the country, causing great hardship for the people left behind.

‹ I ›

Pierre I, Pierre II, and Jonas
1685 to 1730

PIERRE AUMÔNIER was born in 1630 in La Mothe in the province of Haut-Poitou. He was known to have had a brother Jean, who was born between 1635 and 1640. Those were difficult times, but Pierre I, as I will call him, was born with the fire and determination of his parents and grandparents before him, a Protestant who believed in the rights of the Huguenots. There is no record of Pierre's profession. In the early 1650s he married Judith Bonnet, and they had two sons, Pierre II (date of birth unknown) and Jonas, born in 1660. Pierre II became a weaver, and Jonas became a carpenter.

Pierre II married Françoise Biget in or around 1680. He was an active member of Lusignan church and was nominated as church counsellor on 23 June 1680. A few months later, on 23 February 1681, he was appointed, as an Elder of Lusignan church, to represent the parish of Boisgrollier de Rouillé.[1] His continuous strong support of the church did not go unnoticed by the authorities, and in 1681 he was persecuted by the Dragoons. These were Catholic soldiers who hated the Protestants, and they were billeted with Pierre and his family, as they were with many Huguenot families. The dragoons were brutal and insulting, and the wives and children were not spared. Pierre's faith in the Protestant cause did not falter, even though life must have become almost unendurable.

Many Huguenots were massacred for their religious beliefs. Pierre I was shot and killed on the steps of his house in La Mothe in 1685, at about the time of the revocation of the Edict of Nantes. He was fifty-five years old. Born two years after the fall of La Rochelle, he lived through a time of persecution and bloodshed. His brother Jean was murdered in November 1710 at Villedieu de Perron in the parish of Pamproux.

Shortly after the death of their father, Pierre II, his wife Françoise, and Jonas fled to the woods surrounding La Mothe. Leaving behind most of their possessions, they soon began their journey to England. There were many different escape routes. They may have hired a guide or they may have travelled by a route or routes provided by friends who had made successful escapes. Many escaping refugees crossed the Loire river, made their way to Granville on the coast, and from there continued by boat to Jersey and then on to England.[2] If this was the route that Pierre, Françoise, and Jonas took, it would have been a long journey, and as winter approached it would have been difficult and exhausting.

Many escapes failed, and the Huguenots and guides who were caught were severely punished. The men were sent to the galleys, often chained together on their long march to the sea, and the women were frequently confined in convents. Helping or sheltering a Huguenot was a crime punishable by death, and the guides were usually hanged. Some families were separated for years and some were never reunited. The Huguenots were single-minded in their wish to be able to worship freely and were willing to take these appalling risks.[3]

The French refugees spoke little or no English and found the political and social customs in England very different from those in France. Although, for the most part, the Huguenots were well received in England they occasionally met with hostility and even violence. They formed their own communities and established their own churches and, by 1700, there were two distinct communities in London. Weavers and anyone connected with the textile trade lived and worked in Spitalfields, where they could not only find inexpensive housing but where there was less control by the guilds than in central London. And the refugees who were connected with fashion, such as jewellers, hairdressers, and tailors, or the food merchants settled in Westminster and Soho, near the Court and Parliament.[4]

The Huguenots believed that serving God gave meaning to life and they devoted a great deal of their spare time to their churches. There were over twenty French churches in London. They took care of their own poor, and less fortunate refugees were supported through their churches by the Maisons de Charité. In Soho and Spitalfields the Charité distributed meat, bread, soup, vegetables, and occasionally beer.[5]

9

Pierre and Françoise settled in the parish of Shore-ditch, in Spitalfields. At the end of the seventeenth century Spitalfields was surrounded by green fields and rolling pastures. The wooden Elizabethan houses had three or four floors, including the cellar, and the weavers, needing as much light as possible, set up their looms on the top floors where the latticed windows frequently extended the whole width of the house. The looms were extremely noisy and, in an attempt to deaden the sound, they stuffed cotton, silk, or wool waste between the floorboards.[6] The early refugee weavers worked at the house of a master, but by the end of the seventeenth century this had changed, and they frequently took their work home.

By the time Pierre arrived in England the reputation of the Huguenot weavers was well established, and the large demand for cloth provided good employment opportunities for the refugees. The skills that they brought with them, such as the manufacturing of ala-mode silk, had a beneficial affect on the economy in England.[7] By 1695 the weaving trade was flourishing, in part because of an act of Parliament that made it illegal for anyone to wear calicoes or silks imported from India or Persia.

Pierre became a naturalized citizen of Great Britain in 1709,[8] the year the Act of General Naturalization was passed. The fee was one shilling. The Act was for the benefit of foreign Protestants and it demonstrated the government's support of the refugees. There were many advantages: for example, in the weaving trade a foreign master could take an additional apprentice if he became naturalized.

As a foreign weaver Pierre did not have to serve an English apprenticeship, and on 21 March 1715 he was sworn in as a Master of the Weavers Guild.[9] Membership in a French church would certainly have helped his application for admission, but he would also have needed proof that he was a craftsman and that he had left France honestly. A foreign master was required to pay an admission fee of eleven shillings, which was just under a week's earnings for a craftsman working in London at this time. As a Master Weaver Pierre could then take apprentices. His first of record was James Magneron, who began to serve his apprenticeship four years after Pierre became a Master, on 16 February 1719.[10]

Pierre and Françoise had two children: Pierre III, born on 6 April 1702, and Catherine, born on 3 July 1706. Both children were baptized at La Patente church, Spitalfields.

When Pierre III was born Pierre and Françoise were living in Shoreditch. Sometime between the birth of their two children they moved to Stepney, where they lived in Willer Street,[11] situated between Bethnal Green and Whitechapel Road. They probably lived in a brick or stone house. Most of the wooden houses had been destroyed in the Great Fire of 1666 and, by order of Charles II, no more were built. Their house would have been adequately but simply furnished with chests of drawers, a trestle table with a bench or stools, mirrors, and beds with pillows, blankets, and linen. Chairs at this time were very uncomfortable unless they were uphol-stered with horsehair or wool. No household would have been complete without bellows, candlesticks, a smoothing iron, and chamber pots. The cooking uten-sils would have been made of copper, and their dishes may well have been made of pewter.

London, with its smoke and soot, was not a clean city. Indoor plumbing was a rarity, but most of the populace tried to keep clean and washed their hands and faces every day. The old age pensioners in Chelsea would conduct races between the lice they found in their coats and would gamble on the results.[12]

Pierre and Françoise became members of La Pa-tente, Spitalfields, the church that many refugees from the province of Poitou joined. It had been established in 1689. The congregation met at Paternoster Row until 1716, when it moved to a building on Crispin Street.[13] It ceased to exist in 1786 when it merged into the Threadneedle Street congregation. The estimated congregation at the time Pierre and Françoise were members was well over one thousand. At some point they became members of the Church of the Taberna-cle, Glasshouse Street, Leicester Fields, a non-conform-ist church established in 1706 in Westminster. Pierre was an Elder of this church, and his responsibilities would have included membership and finance, authori-zation of baptisms, and distribution of communion to-kens.

‹ ✳ ›

In 1685, when Pierre and Jonas arrived in England, Jonas did not go to London with his brother. He settled in Canterbury, where there was a large community of Huguenots. The Walloons from Belgium and northern France had first settled in the city at the beginning of the seventeenth century, and the French Protestant Huguenots began to settle there in the late 1600s. These new refugees revitalized the city. (There was little difference between the Walloons and the French Huguenots.)

On 10 February 1686 Jonas married Jeanne Fené at the Crypt of Canterbury Cathedral. The marriage was recorded in the church register:

Jonas Aumosnier, fils de Pierre et Judith Bonnet defunt, natif de Poitou pres de St. Mixars, et Jeanne Fené, fille de Pierre Fené, defunt, native de Canterberi, et de Catherine Lancel. Promesse ils ont esté marié en l'église le 10 Fev. 1686–7.[14]

In 1550 Edward VI had, by royal charter, given the Crypt of Canterbury Cathedral to the refugees for their religious assemblies, schools, and meetings. It was a large, cold and gloomy church. Jonas and Jeanne were members of this church and in 1699 Jonas was appointed an Elder and Deacon.[15] As a Deacon he would have maintained church records including the records of the parishioners who were receiving financial assistance from the church.

Jonas and Jeanne had five children: Pierre, born 1687; Jonas, born 1690; Guillaume, born 1693; Jeanne, born 1698; and Daniel, born 1701. They were all baptized at the Church where their parents were married.

Jonas suffered from poor health and in 1701 he moved his family to London, where he died three years later. He was forty-four years old.

Jeanne was not a widow for long. Shortly after Jonas died she married Pierre Marissal, an *ouvrier en soye* (silk weaver), and they lived in Cock Lane in Stepney.[16] By 1705 they had moved to Carters Rents in Stepney, and in 1709 they were living in Red Lion Street. They had four sons.

‹ ✳ ›

Jonas and Jeanne's eldest son, Pierre, became a goldsmith and by 1727 is known to have been in business in St. Anne's, Westminster. On 8 March 1719 he married Suzanne Very at the Church of St. James, Swallow Street. They had three children: Isaac, born 1720; Marie Madeleine, born 1722; and Pierre, born 1729. The children were all christened at the Church of Glasshouse Street and Leicester Fields in Westminster.

There are no further records of this branch of the Aumônier family, the descendants of Jonas.

‹ ✳ ›

In the meantime Pierre II had remarried. Françoise had died (date unknown) and on 29 May 1720 he married Marie Vinuange, a widow, at La Patente, Spitalfields. The marriage was recorded in the church register:

Pierre Aumosnier, homme veuf natif de Cheez en Poitou dem. a Spitalfields et Marie Vinuange, veufue de feu Pierre de Conté.[17]

Pierre died in December 1729.

In 1727 Pierre's daughter, Catherine, married Jacques Charleque at La Patente, Spitalfields. They had two sons and seven daughters. The children were all baptized at the church where their parents were married.

‹ II ›

Mid Eighteenth Century

Pierre III and David

PIERRE III FOLLOWED in the footsteps of his father and grandfather and became a weaver.

The weaving industry continued to thrive in Spitalfields until the middle of the eighteenth century, although calicoes were imported from the East Indies after 1714. London continued to be the principal city for the domestic market, and there was expanding trade with America. Silk designers were also important to the viability of the weaving industry. Fashions changed, and every year there were new patterns for the flowered silks. By the mid 1700s there was a decline in membership of the Weavers Company of London. In the 1720s, when Pierre II first became a weaver, there were 5,954 members, of whom 1,216 were Huguenots, but by 1750 there were 2,531 members and of these only 342 were Huguenots.[1]

On 24 September 1721, when he was nineteen years old, Pierre III married Judith Pigné in the Church of La Patente in Spitalfields,[2] and they lived in Bethnal Green. Judith was the daughter of David Pigné and Marie Bernard. They had six children: Pierre, born

1722, who died in infancy; Marie, born 1724; Bartel-
emy, born 1728; Pierre, born 1733; Abraham, born
1735; and David, born 1739. They were all christened
at La Patente, Spitalfields. Marie married Isaac Robert
at the church of Glasshouse Street and Leicester Fields
on 4 February 1743.

‹ ✱ ›

David, the youngest son, broke away from family tradition and became a shoemaker. In 1755, when he was
sixteen years old, he began to serve an apprenticeship
in Westminster with Peter Goley, a cordwainer. Shoes
were at one time made from cordwain, a leather which
came from Córdoba in Spain and was made from goat
skin.

An indenture which was handwritten on parchment
sets out the terms of David's apprenticeship. In an official document such as this, Pierre III was called Peter
and the English spelling has been adopted for Aumonier.

This indenture Witnesseth that I David Aumonier by and
with the consent of my father Peter Aumonier of St. Matthew's Bethnal Green, Weaver doth put himself Apprentice
to Peter Goley of the Parish of St. Ann's Westminster, Cordwainer to learn his Art and with him after the manner of an
Apprentice to serve from the day of the date hereof unto the
full end and term of Seven years . . . during which term the
said Apprentice, his Master faithfully shall or will serve, his
secrets keep, his lawful commands everywhere gladly do, he
shall do no Damage to his said Master nor see it be done of

others. . . . The Goods of his said Master he shall not waste nor the same without Licence of him to any give or lend. . . . he shall neither buy nor sell without his Master's Licence. Taverns Inns or Alehouses he shall not haunt. At Cards, Dice tables or any other unlawful game he shall not play, nor from the service of his said Master Day or Night absent himself but in all things as an honest and faithful Apprentice shall and will demean and behave himself towards his said master and all his during the said term. And the said Peter Goley in consideration of the faithfull and diligent service of David Aumonier, the said Apprentice, in the Art and mystery of a Cordwainer which he herewith shall teach and instruct or cause to be taught and instructed the best way and manner that he can finding and allowing unto his said Apprentice sufficient Meat, Drink, Washing, Lodging and all other Necessities during the said term (Except Expenses in case of sickness). . . . In Witness whereof the Parties above said to this Indentures interchangeably have set their hands and Seal the Third Day of September in the Thirtieth Year of the reign of our Sovereign Lord George the Second by the Grace of God of Great Britain, France and Ireland King Defender of the Faith and in the Year of our Lord One Thousand Seven hundred and fifty five.[3]

David lived with the Goley family, who probably lived above or behind the business. Peter Goley was married to a Marie Aumônier, who may have been related to David. (There is no record of her parentage.[4]) Living in the centre of London would have been very different from living in Bethnal Green, on the outskirts of the city, where David had lived for the greater part of his childhood. London was growing rapidly and was crowded, noisy, dirty, and not particularly safe. Houses and shops were close together, the cobbled streets were narrow, and pedestrians and carriages jostled against each other. A gutter for slops and filth ran down the middle of the street. And then there was the noise—the horses' hooves, the iron-covered wheels on the carriages, the shouting tradesmen, the rowdy patrons of the taverns and coffee-houses, and the street vendors singing traditional verses and selling everything from dog meat to ribbons to chimney-sweeping. The tradesmen's signs were another hazard. Large and heavy and hung on iron brackets, they frequently fell, injuring or killing the pedestrians walking below. Under an Act of Parliament passed in 1762 this type of signboard became illegal in the Cities of London and Westminster.

An apprentice's day was a long one. David probably worked twelve to fourteen hours a day beginning at six o'clock in the morning. By the end of the day he had little energy for anything other than climbing the stairs and going to bed. The main meal, dinner, was eaten in the middle of the day and for supper there were the left-overs.

During his apprenticeship David became proficient in making shoes for both men and women. Men's shoes, in the mid eighteenth century, were made of black or dark brown leather and had square toes and buckles. Shoes with red heels were sometimes worn for formal occasions. By 1770 the toes had become sharply pointed, and red heels were not restricted to evening wear. Light-coloured leathers, such as white and yellow, came into fashion at the end of the century. Women's shoes were made of light brocade, satin, wool, or linen depending on the occasion and the time of year: wool was best for winter wear and linen cool in the summer. Shoes were usually lined with white kid, and the plainer materials were often decorated with braiding, lace, or embroidery. Toes were pointed, and heels, which varied, were frequently rather thick and Baroque, although it was fashionable to totter in the ballroom. In 1762 the *London Chronicle* reported: "As to their shoe heels, ladies go just as they did, some as broad as a tea-cup's brim and some as narrow as the china circle the cup stands on." In bad weather women wore galoshes over their shoes or fitted decorative clogs. Leather shoes did not become fashionable for women until the end of the eighteenth century. In the seventeenth century and most of the eighteenth, men and women both wore very high heels and shoes were made with a straight last. To keep the shape of a straight shoe walkers were advised not to wear the same shoe on the same foot on consecutive days, but to alternate them. Right and left shoes were reintroduced in 1790 with the return of flat shoes.[5]

By the mid 1760s David was working for Peter Bourdon, who had a large business and employed twenty-six men. He was a patriotic man who was sympathetic to the Huguenot cause, as were his employees.[6] Mrs. Bourdon is said to have given £57 8*s* to the French Protestant School of Westminster between the years 1765 and 1768. The Huguenots had established boarding and day schools for the refugee children, but little is known about these schools. In English schools the boys, but not the girls, were taught arithmetic as soon as they could read and write; the girls were taught needlework, spinning, and knitting. Religious instruction and the teaching of morals were important parts of the curriculum.

In 1765, when he was twenty-six years old, David married Peter Bourdon's daughter Anne. They lived in Wheeler Street, possibly in the same house that David's father had lived in as a child (Pierre II had lived in "Willer street" but there were several variants of the name including Willow, Wellers, Whiller, Wheeler and Wheler). On 25 January 1766 David presented "témoignage" to the French church in Threadneedle Street, where he had applied for membership. Témoignage was a document brought from the previous church of membership, usually by new refugees, and it certified faith and good behavior.[7] David and Anne had eight children: Pierre, born 1766, who died in infancy; Jean, born 1768; Anne, born 1770; Pierre, born 1772; David, born 1773; Philippe, born 1776; Jacques, born 1777; and Mary Ann, born 1785.

As a shoemaker David was able to provide adequately for his family. In 1718 his father earned about three shillings a day, but by 1760 the wages would have been higher. In 1767 meat cost threepence to fourpence a pound, bread twopence a pound, and cheese threepence-halfpenny a pound. They would have eaten mutton, beef, pork, cheeses, apple puddings, and jellies, and on special occasions they may have had roast partridge or roast swan.

‹ * ›

Jean, David and Anne's oldest living son, became a jeweller and goldsmith (see Chapter III), and David, their third son, became a stockbroker. David did not marry; he is known to have lived near the Sadlers Wells Theatre in St. John's Road, and later in Penton Place, Pentonville.[8]

‹ * ›

Mary Ann, David and Anne's youngest daughter, lived with her brother Jean and his wife Mary for a short while in the early 1800s. On 12 October 1806 she married William Woollams at St. James' Church, Paddington.

William Woollams was a paperstainer.[9] He served his apprenticeship first with John Sherringham, a paperstainer in great Marlborough Street, and then, for the last fifteen months, probably as a result of Mr. Sherringham's death, with George Cook of New Road. He then worked as a journeyman in Chelsea, and later for his brother John, also a paperstainer. In 1806 or 1807, shortly after his marriage to Mary Ann, William started his own painting, paperstaining, and decorating business at 31 Wigmore Street, Cavendish Square, where he had a 'table,' that is, a paperstaining press for printing wallpaper, in the front kitchen. He also had a paperstaining workshop in Jew's Harp Yard near Albany

Street (now part of Regents Park) and in 1837 he established a factory at 110 High Street, Marylebone. Mary Ann printed the first piece of wallpaper produced in the factory. Woollams and Company specialized in high-quality hand-printed wallpaper and was, in the nineteenth century, one of the leading manufacturers of wallpaper in London.[10]

Mary Ann and William had twelve children: Mary-Anne, born 1807; William, born 1809; Thomas, born 1812; John, born 1816; Henry, born 1818; David, born 1824; Frederick, born 1827; and Emily, born 1829. (Three daughters and one son died in infancy).

Mary Ann and William's marriage was the beginning of a relationship between the two families that would continue for several generations. Emily, their youngest daughter, married her first cousin Frederick Gibson Aumonier, son of Mary Ann's brother Jean, and two of Jean's grandsons were apprenticed to William Woollams and Company (see Chapters IV and V).

William Woollams died in 1840, and his business continued under the management of three of his sons, William, Thomas, and Henry. William became the senior partner. Thomas, who was not particularly interested in the manufacturing side of the business, sold his share to his two brothers in 1852. The three brothers all married, but William and Henry did not have children. William married Sophia Green in the late 1840s, and Henry married Elizabeth Nisbet in 1844; Thomas married Mary Anne Reid in 1842 and they had three sons and one daughter.

William died in 1859 and Henry became sole proprietor of William Woollams and Company. In his will William left money in trust for his mother Mary Ann, providing her with an annuity of £100. She died on 26 December of the following year.

Henry was very fond of his Aumonier cousins and had a great sense of family and social responsibility. When he died in 1876 he left legacies to many relatives, including his Aumonier cousins, to various friends, and also to hospitals. His estate was valued at just under £50,000.

‹ III ›

John and Mary

A Love Match

JEAN, DAVID AND ANNE'S oldest son, was fourteen and a half years old when he began to serve a seven-year apprenticeship with Philip Holmes Wisher, a jeweller and goldsmith, of the Parish of St. Giles, in Spitalfields. The indenture was signed on 13 January 1783 by John and his two brothers Peter and Jack (by this time all the brothers had adopted the English spelling of their names), but not by Philip Holmes Wisher.

The terms and conditions of an apprenticeship were much the same in 1783 as they had been in 1755, when David had begun his. The only notable difference is that John was not allowed to marry during his apprenticeship: "[he] shall not commit Fornication, nor contract Matrimony within the said Term."

Although there is no record of John's becoming a member of the Guild of the London Goldsmiths, nor of his being granted a hallmark, he would have needed to complete both these formalities before he could begin working as a goldsmith and jeweller. To obtain a hallmark a goldsmith had to produce a piece of work, usually called a masterpiece. Hallmarking was introduced to prevent fraud, and a goldsmith who sold, exchanged, or exported a piece before it was tested and marked was subject to a penalty of £50 plus forfeiture of the piece or pieces. From 1720 to 1757 and from 1784 to 1790 the duty on silver made in England was sixpence per troy ounce. This had to be paid by the silversmith at the local assay office.[1]

In the eighteenth century jewellery was light and delicate with the fragility of lace. As evening entertainment became fashionable, women wanted pieces that would sparkle in the candlelight.

During his apprenticeship John lived with Mr. and Mrs. Wisher, and he probably continued to work for Mr. Wisher and live with the family after he completed his training. There is no record of the date of Philip Holmes Wisher's death, but it appears that Mrs. Wisher was a widow by the spring of 1793, for on 31 March John took over the business in partnership with a Mr. Gibson and a Mr. Faust. On 30 March he wrote to his fiancée Mary Everard:

My affairs are at last come to a determination & (if I may be permitted to express myself in a figurative way) I am on the eve of embarking on the main Ocean, in a very small vessel, & trust to Providence to crown my endeavours with success, & to direct me so to steer my course that I may at last arrive at the Harbour of Prosperity. I shall I doubt not have many difficulties to surmount, but I trust through the blessing of God I shall get over them.

Mrs. Wisher agreed to move out of the house, and John, who was not used to housekeeping, realized that he and his two partners would need a servant. He interviewed a woman who was "neither young nor pretty as it might be dangerous in a house with single men."[2] There is no record of whether he hired her or not, but Mrs. Wisher did not move out as planned and was still living in the house in July.

John had many worries in the summer of 1793. England was at war with France, which "makes business in my line very slack," his beloved Mary had been ill, and in July "the house was broken open in the night . . . and robbed of property to a considerable amount." He is philosophical "all things have but a time. . . . I never despaired yet & I will not begin now."[3]

John met Mary Everard in 1791 or 1792. She was born in 1771 and was the daughter of William and Mary Everard. She is known to have had a brother, Will. In 1793 Mary lived and may have worked at Miss Symon's boarding school in Wantage, Berkshire. She and John were engaged and they wrote to each other frequently. A few of John's letters remain. They are an expression of his love and devotion, but he also wrote about the family and friends, social occasions, and sometimes the weather.

London, March 30 1793

Dear Mary

I cannot begin this epistle better than by expressing my Gratitude and thanking you a thousand times for your kind condescension in answering my letter as soon as you did. . . . I hope that I shall be indulged with another letter from you. You cannot imagine in what spirits (the kind expressions and confessions you made in your last) put me in. I was quite enraptured, & kissed the paper over & over again for being the means of conveying those kind sentiments to me, and eagerly wish[d] for the dear original that I might clasp you in my arms, & prove to you how much I Love and how grateful I am to you for having so generously promised to keep your Heart for me, I shall make it my study if possible to deserve it. O my dear Girl continue but this kind & I shall have reason to bless the hour when I first became acquainted with you. I am proud to own I love you & am happy I have fixt my love on so worthy an object, believe me sincere. I hope I shall hear from you soon and that you will not use any reserve but write to me generous & open and give full scope to your ideas, depend on it I will repay your kindness with gratitude. . . . Adieu my dearest Love may you enjoy all the happiness I think you are deserved of & may I be enabled to reward your constancy by placing you in a situation wherein you may be comfortable is the sincere wish of

Your Lover & Friend
J. Aumonier.

On 22 May he wrote:

O my dear Mary how I wish to see you. I hope you will not resolve on not coming to town in Midsummer but that my eyes may be blest with the sight of my lovely Girl all fresh and blooming as my imagination anticipates she is—every moment of absence to a true lover seems an hour. I certainly find it so—believe the sincerity of my affection are not in the least abated—on the contrary they are increased by the kindness you express[d] in you Letter rely on it I do not flatter you in mine.

In the late eighteenth century it was not unusual for middle-class Londoners to take holidays in the countryside surrounding London. There were Clapham, Stock-well, and Camberwell to the south, Kensington in the west and Hampstead in the north. In May 1793 John went to Stockwell for a few days. It was the weekend of the Stockwell Fair, and Mary's brother Will and his wife and children were in town, as were one of John's brothers and Mr. & Mrs. L'Homme. Mrs. L'Homme may have been John's aunt, the sister of his mother Anne Bourdon, although this cannot be confirmed. (Marie Bourdon was married to Guillaume L'Homme and they had four children.[4]) In his letter of 7 July 1793 John writes "Mrs. L'Homme's protuberance begins to get very perceptible. I think it will not be very long before I have a new cousin." In March Mr. and Mrs. L'Homme had "engaged lodgings for the summer season at Mr. Powels," but John wrote "I believe her stay there will not be long, Mrs. Cole & Mrs. Wisher did lodge in the same house but all the people who belong to it are so uncivil that they only stayed there a week." John was well entertained. He dined with Mary's brother Will and his wife on May 20 and the following day at "Mrs. L's with a large party of Friends." Everybody had a good time, "Stockwell was all alive it was fair time there were different sorts of amusements going forward—Jingling Matches, Running in Sacks, Cudgelling &c &c. We passed a very agreeable day."[5]

Mary was ill at the beginning of the summer and did not go to London to see John and her family. John was very concerned; he imagined the worst. She writes to John as soon as she is better and he replies on 7 July:

I received yours of the 20th of June. I opened it trembling, but my joy overpayed my anxiety, when I read the contents; how uneasy have I been about you, but I thank God that my fears are now subsided. Had you not wrote you would have seen me at Wantage before this time. I wrote to your Father and Mrs. L'Homme immediately after I read you letter to inform them of the good news and put an end to their apprehensions which I assure you were of the worst sort. Your friends care and anxiety for you is very great & can only be equal[d] by your Duty to them, for I am persuaded you will never lose sight of filial gratitude.

I have been longer this time in writing to you than I intended, but I wished to see your Friends before I wrote and had no opportunity until last night, but the delay of a week I trust will be overlooked. . . .

Your Father and Mother are well at present but their uneasiness for you made them rather unwell before they heard from you. They both send their loves to you and your Mother requests you will write particularly to her & let her know the particulars of your illness, & as you do not come home these Holidays begs you to send word when you will come, for she is very anxious to see you. . . . I wish much to see you & however imprudent you may think it I believe I shall not overcome the desire I have to see you at Wantage. I give you this hint that you may not be surprised at seeing me there. I suppose your Nunnery is not altogether inaccessible especially as a great part of the Nuns are gone for a time and hope then I shall have the pleasure of seeing you speaking to you touching you & kissing you and—but I must stop here & not let my raptures carry me too far. O my Dear Girl you employ my thoughts by Day and Dreams by Night & the pleasing hope of being happy in making you so buoys me up above the trifling misfortunes I experience.

He continued with family news,

> Your brothers and sisters send their love to you. William's [Mary's brother] eldest girl is just recovered from the smallpox and the youngest girl just taken it, but seems to be in a fair way of doing well. He and his wife are well so is Frederick & his family. I believe you forgot to make the enquiry for which I desired you in one of my Letters to do. Mr. & Mrs. L'Homme desire their love to you. They are well but very busy as he is just entering into business for himself, and making great alterations in the house. . . . Little Mary [L'Homme] grows a very fine girl I may say very pretty, she is very engaging and if I could have a child formed according to my own mind I would take pattern from her. . . . The Weather is so intensely hot that it quite relaxes me and I can scarcely write or do any thing else. . . . Adieu, may you enjoy all the happiness I think you deserve & then your life will be pleasant indeed.

John and Mary were married on 14 March 1795 at St. Mary's Church, Islington. The church registry recorded the witnesses of the marriage as David Aumonier and Mary L'Homme. They had six children: Frances Anne, born 1796; Alfred Everard, born 1797; John Henry Collingwood, born 1799; Frederic Gibson, born 1801; John William, born 1803, and David, born 1811. Frances Anne and Alfred Everard died in childhood. The four oldest children were baptized at the Church of St. Jean in Spitalfields, and John William and David were baptized at St. George the Martyr in Southwark. This was the first generation that recorded more than one name at baptism, and both John Henry Collingwood and Frederick Gibson were given, as middle names, the last names of their godparents. John Henry Collingwood's godparents were David Aumonier and Frances Collingwood, and Frederic Gibson's godparents were James and Mary Gibson.[6]

By 1796 John had a jewellery business at 19 Denmark Street, Soho, and in 1797 he took a Mr. Faust into partnership at this address.

Mary died on 28 April 1819. She was forty-eight years old. After twenty-four years of marriage John was still very much in love with Mary, and an *Epitaph to the memory of Mary Aumonier by Him who best knew her worth*, signed with the initials "JA," is attributed to John.

> Take sacred earth all that my soul held dear
> Take that best gift which Heaven in beauty gave
> Long time I daily marked with grief sincere
> Her faiding form, but had not power to save.
> As Mother, Wife, or Friend beloved rever'd
> By Parents Husband children was ador'd,
> By every tie that binds the Heart endear'd
> In life respected, and in Death deplor'd.
> Does Youth, does Beauty read these lines.
> Does simpathetic fear their breasts alarm,
> Speak, my Dead Mary, breathe a strain Divine.
> E'en from the grave thou canst have power to charm,
> Bid them be chaste be innocent like thee.
> Bid them in duties paths as humbly move
> And if so fair, from vanity is free
> As firm in friendship and as fond in Love
> Tell them Tho' 'twas an awful thing to die
> 'Twas e'en to thee—Yet the dread path once trod

Heaven lifts its everlasting portals High
And bids the pure in Heart behold their God.

By 1825 John and his youngest son David were living near Hampstead Road in the Parish of St. Pancras in north London. David was eight years old when his mother died. John died on 13 March 1834, a few months before his sixty-sixth birthday.

‹ IV ›

The Jewellers

Henry, Frederic, and David

JOHN HENRY COLLINGWOOD, Frederic Gibson, and David all followed in their father's footsteps and became goldsmiths and jewellers. There is no record of either Henry's or Frederic's apprenticeships. The three brothers had a close business relationship over the years and David served part of his apprenticeship with Henry.

It is apparent that Henry quickly established himself as a jeweller and goldsmith. His first business was at 58 King Street in Soho, and on 23 June 1828 he entered his mark, HA, at Goldsmiths' Hall under the name Henry Collingwood Aumonier.[1] He was also a member of the Jewellers Society.

In the mid nineteenth century jewellery was for the most part produced by craftsmen in their workshops, although a few small jewellery factories had been established. Jewellers created their own designs, frequently drawing their inspiration from the medieval and Renaissance periods. An example of this enthusiasm for the past was the ferronnière, which was composed of a chain or cord tied around the head with a single jewel

34

hanging in the centre of the forehead. Jewellery was an important accessory and became a way a young woman could show her personality and individuality. Bow-shaped brooches and bracelets and heart-shaped lockets were popular, as were friendship rings decorated with flowers, a loving message, or a picture of one's beloved. In this age of sentimentality it was not uncommon to see a brooch or ring with hair as part of the design or placed in a small receptacle at the back of the piece. Cameos were also popular; they were cut in onyx, sardonyx or agate, and inexpensive reproductions could be made in shell or glass. Turquoise was in fashion, as were pearls, pink topaz, emeralds, diamonds, and sapphires. A woman who could not afford gold jewellery set with precious stones could buy attractive and fashionable jewellery made with paste, inexpensive stones such as coral and jet, or marcasite. Henry's jewellery designs frequently included flowers: they were charming, delicate and fashionable. Several of his sketches have survived, including one of a bracelet of intertwining flowers and another of drop-earrings with a flower.

On 6 June 1827, when he was twenty-eight years old, Henry married Nancy Frances Stacy. Nancy was eight years younger than Henry. They had eight children: Henry Stacy, born 1828; George, born 1829, who died in early childhood; James, born 1832; Nancy, born 1834, who died in infancy; Emma, born 1835; Frederick, born 1837; William, born 1839; and Louise, born 1846. The children were all baptized at St. Dunstan in the West, the church where their parents were married.

When they were first married Henry and Nancy probably lived above or behind the business at 58 King Street. By 1830 they had moved to 41 Frith Street, also in Soho, and by 1834 Henry was in business in Lower Ashby Street. In the early 1840s his brother David was also in business in Lower Ashby Street.[2]

The nineteenth century was a time of change and progress. London was still a dirty and noisy city although less crowded than it had been in the previous century. In addition to private carriages there were horse-drawn trams, omnibuses, cabs, and errand-boys on horseback. There were open sewers, and cholera was as common as smallpox. Between 1831 and 1866 there were four cholera epidemics in England. As a result of the Municipal Corporations Act of 1845 and the Public Health Act of 1848, water supplies in the cities and towns improved, and sewers were built.

The development of the railway changed the pattern of life for many people. They could now travel for pleasure and, if they chose, live at some distance from their places of work. The first passenger train line, the Stockton and Darlington, opened in 1825, and the first long distance line, from London to Birmingham, opened in 1830. An Act of Parliament passed in 1844 regulated the frequency of railway service to at least one train a day on every line at a fare of one penny a mile for adults and half-fare for children between the ages of three and twelve. The rides may not have been very comfortable but that was secondary to reaching one's destination.

Railway stocks were widely promoted and became a source of wealth for anyone willing to take the risk of investing in one of the new railway companies. An example of this type of investment is seen in the will of Henry Woollams, the first cousin of Henry, Frederic, and David. His investments included the London and North Western Railway, the Metropolitan District Railway, the North Metropolitan Tramway, and the East Indian Railway Company. It was not until the end of the century that railways were owned and financed on a national level.

In the late 1830s Henry and Nancy moved out of London to Highgate, a little way to the north, and by the early 1840s they were living in Hertfordshire, at Waterloo House in Barnet. This was also Henry's business address.

By 1844 Henry had expanded his business: in addition to being a jeweller and goldsmith he was also a dealer in foreign and English needlework. He created needle-point designs on canvas and calico and he stocked the silks and wools needed for embroidery. He also made the dyes that were needed to imprint the design on to the fabric. He noted his method of making Brunswick Green: "To a solution of sulphate of copper, [add] bilastarch of potass, stirring the whole well together until the original blue colour is destroyed. . . . This when treated in the usual way is an inferior Brunswick green." A balance sheet for Waterloo House, dated 6 August 1844, is signed "FA" and its preparation is attributed to Henry's brother Frederic. It appears that the two brothers had a business association in the early 1840s, as the balance sheet contains two entries that refer to FA; one for bills that he accepted and another for cash in the amount of £263.

Henry and Nancy discovered that living in the country was not always easy. They had a troublesome neighbour, Mr. Leather, who allowed his fowl to wander onto their land. Henry decided to take the matter in hand:

March 21, 1846

Dear Sir

I have lately taken part of Mr. Walker's ground which I am attempting to convert into a garden, but find it so over run with vermin of all sorts, that I am compelled in my own defence to destroy them if possible. I think it therefore right, to caution you, as regards your Fowls, who are in the daily habit of paying me a visit, (damaging, and destroying in one half hour, what has taken me much time to get up) that if after this they should come, they may chance to pick up, what will not at all agree with them, and I cannot answer for the consequences. Mr. Courtnall, and Mr. Walker, who are both equally annoyed in the same way, I believe intend to adopt the same course, if therefore you have any respect for your Fowls you will adopt means to keep them upon your own premises.

It is not known if Henry carried out his threats.

Henry's health began to fail in the late 1840s and he died two weeks before his forty-ninth birthday, on 17 March 1848. His funeral was on Sunday 26 March 1848 at two o'clock in the afternoon, and he was buried in Highgate Cemetery (grave 2678). Henry Stacy, his eldest son, had chosen the site for the grave a few days earlier, on 21 March. The Cemetery and General Funeral Company were responsible for the funeral arrangements, and their bill (£26 1s) included such items as "Extra distance for Patent Carriage and 4, Mourning Coach, two pairs of Town made Kid Gloves, Watering Horses and turnpikes." A marble headstone with curb and iron railing was erected over the grave in June. The receipt for the headstone and the bill from the Cemetery and General Funeral Company are both signed by W. L'Homme.[3]

After Henry died Nancy moved to Belvedere Road in Upper Norwood in Surrey where she died in 1856, at the age of forty-seven years. She was buried beside Henry. Their daughter Emma, who died in 1869, was also buried in this grave.

‹ * ›

In 1844 Frederic went into business with John James Robinson, a jeweller and goldsmith, at 153 Leadenhall Street in London, and John James Robinson & Co. became Robinson & Aumonier. There had been a goldsmith, silversmith, and jewellery business at this address since the end of the eighteenth century. The partnership lasted until John James Robinson's retirement on 10 March 1849. The business was renamed Frederic Aumonier, and Frederic continued on his own as a goldsmith and electroplate manufacturer. He was licensed to value gold and silver plate, jewellery, diamonds, and precious stones. Following his death in

1866 the business was called Aumonier & Co. and remained that way until 1873.[4]

In 1851 Frederic, as was mentioned at the end of Chapter II, married his first cousin Emily Woollams, the youngest daughter of William Woollams and Mary Ann Aumonier. Emily was twenty-two years old, twenty-eight years younger than Frederic. A marriage settlement setting up a trust in connection with Emily's inheritance from her father William Woollams was signed on 5 May 1851, three days before the wedding.

Frederic and Emily lived at 153 Leadenhall Street behind or above the business. They were an hospitable couple, and Emily surrounded herself with friends, mostly people from the theatre. She was also reputed to be an inveterate matchmaker, and several young couples were "afforded the opportunity to carry that courtship to a happy ending under her husband's hospitable roof!" It is said that Emily was terrified of thunderstorms, and in 1847 when she and her mother were staying at Waterloo House with Henry and Nancy, there was a terrible thunderstorm and she "in mortal terror hid herself in the coal cellar."[5]

Frederic and Emily did not have any children, but they adopted Emily's niece Harriette Emily Woollams, the eldest daughter of her brother John. Harriette was born in 1842, nine years before Emily and Frederic were married. She developed a fine contralto voice and played and sang with the D'Oyly Carte Company under the name of Miss Everard, the maiden name of her great-aunt Mary.

Frederic died in 1866 and was buried in Highgate Cemetery (grave 14869). He was sixty-five years old. Emily moved back to King Street, Portman Square, where she had lived with her mother before her marriage. She later moved to Duke Street, Manchester Square, where her niece Adela, also a daughter of her brother John, lived with her as a companion. Emily received a residuary legacy of £4,025 under the will of her brother Henry Woollams, who died in 1876. Emily was a widow for thirteen years and died on 7 March 1879 at the age of fifty. She was buried beside her husband Frederic on 24 March. Harriette, who died in 1882, was also buried in this grave.

‹ ✳ ›

John William, John and Mary's third son, was two years younger than Frederic. Little is known about him. On 24 July 1823 he married Ann Elizabeth Collop at St. Margaret's Westminster, and they lived in Tonbridge Street in London. He was only twenty years old while Ann Elizabeth, who had been born on 19 January 1796, was twenty-seven. They had five children: Mary Ann, born 1824; Elizabeth Frances, born 1827; Ann Elizabeth, born 1828; John, born 1829, who died in infancy; and Emily Sarah, born 1832, who also died in infancy. John died on 23 November 1833, and his widow subsequently married a Mr. Foshay, who was four years her senior.

Under the will of Henry Woollams, Mary Ann and

Elizabeth Frances both received £250. Ann Elizabeth predeceased Henry.

‹ ✳ ›

David, the youngest of the brothers, was eight years old when his mother Mary died, and by 1825 he and his father were living near Hampstead Road in the Parish of St. Pancras in north London. Five days after his fourteenth birthday, on 25 April 1825, David began to serve an apprenticeship with John Greswell, a goldsmith and jeweller, who had his business at 21 Portland Street in London.[6] Under the terms of the indenture John Greswell was paid "the sum of Twenty nine pounds of lawful money of Great Britain."

In 1831 Mr. Greswell emigrated to Perth, Australia.[7] The year before, on 25 May 1830, it was agreed:

by mutual consent . . . to dissolve the contact or contracts contained in this indenture of apprenticeship and the said indenture is thereby rendered void.

David had served five years of his apprenticeship. He served the last two years with his brother Henry in Frith Street in Soho. The new contract was very brief:

David Aumonier of No. 21 Portland Street Soho and Henry Aumonier of 41 Frith Street Soho do agree that the article of apprenticeship contained in this indenture shall continue in force between them in every respect as between the said David Aumonier and the above John Gresswell. Henry Aumonier holding by [illegible] consent the place of John Gresswell.

42

On 24 July 1838 David married Ann Maria Butler at Trinity Church in Marylebone. They had nine children: Maria Louise, born 1839; Fanny Caroline, born 1840; David Edward, born 1841; Charles John, born 1843; Laura Mary, born 1845; Francis Henry, born 1850; Elizabeth Emily, who died at birth, and Caroline, twins born 1857; and Arthur, born 1861.

For a brief period in the early 1840s David was in business in Lower Ashby Street with Henry. He then went into business by himself at 42 Wigmore Street. This, however, was not a successful venture, and he decided to move his family to Liverpool, where they lived in Cases Street. Henry wanted to help his brother and he wrote to an old acquaintance (there is no record of the recipient) who lived in Liverpool:

Although a lapse of twenty years has probably elapsed since you and I met, you may perhaps remember my name by carrying your recollection back to the friendly society held at Angel, High Street, Bloomsbury, London where we have spent many a pleasant evening together—if you should not have forgotten me and the terms of friendship upon which we then stood, I know that you will readily accede to the trifling request I am about to make for old acquaintance sake. I have a brother who has come down to Liverpool with his wife and family upon the chance of getting a living as a working jeweller. He is a good general hand and particularly handy at jobbing. He undertakes the hair work, guard chains, &c and I think will be found a very useful man to the good folks of Liverpool if he can establish himself. The request therefore I have to make is that if you can put any thing in his way in the way of business either personally or by recommendation you will do so, and by so doing you will confer a favour upon an old acquaintance, and I trust have no cause to regret serving an industrious man to whom dame fortune has not been particularly kind of late.

Ann Maria took up hairdressing to help support their growing family. By 1855 David and Ann Maria were living at 35 Mulberry Street, Mount Pleasant, Liverpool, and David had found steady employment with a Mr. Mayers, who was probably a jeweller and appears to have had a fairly large business with thirteen employees.

David kept in touch with the family in London. On 29 December 1855 he wrote to his nephew James, an artist whom we shall meet in the next chapter:

I received your Christmas Cartoon we are all much obliged and am happy to say we did manage to spend a merry day. . . . We have all been to the Exhibition and seen your Picture which meets with general admiration. I think it very good indeed and I think you are fortunate in having it in a very good place. It is in the principal room which is Octagon shape so of course it is in one of the angles, it would have been better rather lower but still it is in a good place. I cannot say so much for your friends pictures they are all badly placed in out of the way corners where *you cannot see the defects*. . . . I am still working for Mr. Mayers he gave us all a very sumptuous feed in first class style on the 1st of Dec. . . . We all had a fright in the shop the other night. The front shop closes at 6 in the evening and we work until seven to that after six all is closed in the front and we have to go out down a back stair case something like a chimney our workshop being on the second floor. At about ¹/₂ past-six, after the

44

shop had closed, there was a fire in the building. It began in the packing cases and straw stored in the cellar and we were all aroused with a cry of fire! Of course we all rushed out into the passage where the staircase our only egress was all in a blaise and the smoke suffocating. However some of them got a crazy old ladder and we managed to get down to the roof of the showroom at the back and by this time the alarm was given and the firemen soon extinguished it. . . . The fire began in the cellar under the staircase which is full of Packing cases and straw &c fortunately no damage was done to the show shop.

David established himself with some success in Liverpool and he remained there for the rest of his life. In 1876 he received a pecuniary legacy of £500 under the will of his cousin Henry Woollams.

David died in 1886 at the age of seventy-five.

His oldest son, David Edward, worked for the *Liverpool Mercury* as a compositor. In 1870 David Edward married Lucy June Mitchell and they had four children: William, born 1871; Mary Louise, born 1873; Charles, born 1876; and Thomas Frederick, born 1879. Thomas Frederick and his son John Charles were both members of the Liverpool Stock Exchange.

David and Ann Maria had many other grandchildren. One of them, Henry Francis Butler, the son of Francis Henry, published a book of poems in 1953.[8]

‹ ✳ ›

Six of Henry and Nancy's seven children survived to adulthood: Henry Stacy, James (see Chapter V), Emma, who died in 1869, Frederick (always known as Fred), William (see Chapter VI), and Louise. They were successful, creative, and artistic.

‹ ✳ ›

Henry Stacy became an engineer and toolmaker and had a successful business in Clerkenwell. One of his apprentices was his second cousin Fred Woollams, the son of Thomas. In this generation there is further evidence of the strong bond that existed between the Aumonier and the Woollams families.

In 1861 Henry Stacy married Susan Foote, and they had five sons and two daughters: Harry, born 1861; George, born 1863; Charles Stacy, born 1866; Ernest, born 1867; Sidney, born 1869; Alice Maud, born 1870; and Kate, born 1874. The family lived in Leyton, which was fairly near Henry's business in Clerkenwell. In 1876 Henry received £250 under the will of Henry Woollams.

Henry Stacy was a kind and loving husband and father and enjoyed the simple things in life. He died on 16 January 1917, three months before his ninetieth birthday, and was buried in the family grave in Highgate Cemetery (grave 2678).

‹ ✳ ›

Fred went into the paperstaining and wallpaper business. In 1853, when he was sixteen years old, he went to work for his father's cousins William and Henry Woollams at the paperstaining factory in Marylebone. Fred probably served an apprenticeship for the first seven years, but this cannot be confirmed. He lived in Broad Court in Covent Garden, where his brothers James and William also lived in the mid 1850s.

Fred remained with William Woollams and Company his entire working life, and when Henry Woollams died in 1876 he purchased the business. By this time Fred was a widower. His first wife June Shaw, whom he married in 1864, died in 1875. In his will Henry left Fred a pecuniary legacy of £1,000. Henry and his wife were childless, and they may have had an agreement with Fred that he would take over the business upon Henry's death. In 1877 Fred married Elizabeth Sutcliffe and they had one son, Frederick, born 1879. They lived in Harrow.

William Woollams and Company was a highly successful business and received many awards over the years. It produced a variety of wallpapers but was particularly well-known for floral designs. The firm first used steam cylinder printing in 1849 and showed both block- and machine-printed wallpaper at the Great Exhibition of 1851. In 1877 Fred developed a process for making embossed flock papers, which he patented, and he also developed pigments that were free of arsenic.[9]

The factory closed in 1900.[10]

In 1910 the younger Frederick married Mary Lewis and they had a son, Frederick John, born 1911.

‹ * ›

Louise, Henry and Nancy's youngest daughter, was a watercolour artist. She usually painted flowers, and her floral designs were used by William Woollams and Company for its hand blocked-chintz papers.[11] Louise received £250 under the will of Henry Woollams.

Louise exhibited at the Royal Academy and several London galleries. Her paintings *Caper Gathered from the Ancient Walls of Rome, Hollyhocks of Kew Gardens,* and *Chrysanthemums* were shown at the Royal Academy in 1895, *Sunflowers* in 1897, and *February Posies* in 1900. She also exhibited at the New Water-colour Society, the Grafton Gallery, the Royal Society of British Artists, the Royal Institute of Painters in Water-colours, the Royal Institute of Oil Painters, and the Royal Hibernian Academy.[12]

Louise married Alfred Warner. She died on 17 October 1901 at the age of forty-five.

‹ V ›

James

1832 to 1911

JAMES' INTEREST in painting began at a very early age. As a child growing up in Highgate and Barnet he would go into the garden and try to draw or paint the flowers. In those early days, he said, "the strength of my water-colours . . . consisted of a lump of gamboge [gum resin from Cambodian and Siamese trees used as yellow pigment], a cake of Prussian blue and one of crimson lake. . . . I had very great delight in producing what my father called 'good fat green' by mixing the gamboge and the Prussian blue together—that was my only green."[1] When he was ready to experiment with oils a kindly neighbour, who was the village carriage painter, gave him some oil paints in a variety of colours. He bought a camel-hair brush for a penny and, copying from an engraving, painted a picture of *Old Barking Church*.

James had to have a profession, and it was decided that he should become a paperstainer. His father's cousins Henry and William Woollams agreed to take him as an apprentice and he began his training on 9 April 1846, his fourteenth birthday. The apprentice's working day was shorter in the mid 1800s than it had been one hundred years previously and he did not have to live with the master. Under the terms of the indenture Henry and William Woollams agreed to pay James:

during the first year of the said Term . . . the sum of six shillings per week by way of wages, the second year . . . the sum of seven shillings per week, the third year the sum of nine shillings per week and payable weekly in each year and for the remainder of the said Term of Seven years pay and allow their said Apprentice the half of his weekly earning but in case of illness of their said apprentice and his inability to work during any portion of the said first three years of the said Term then during such illness no wages shall be paid to their said apprentice.

There is no record of where James lived during the first few years of his apprenticeship, but by the mid 1850s he was living in Broad Court, Covent Garden. His younger brother Frederick lived at this address in 1853, the year he began working at the paperstaining factory, and William, the youngest brother, moved in two years later. This was probably a boarding-house, as Fred and William were sixteen years old when they first lived there. By 1856 James was living at 13 Upper York Street, Bryanston Square.

James did not like working at the paperstaining factory but tried to make the best of it. In the evenings he studied drawing at the Mechanics Institute.[2] The classes were held in an old, poorly lit lecture room. There was a gas lamp over the instructor's table, and the Institute provided candlesticks and snuffers for the students, who had to bring their own candles. And so James learned to draw in a room lit by small pools of flickering candlelight. He was a diligent student, and when he had learned all he could at the Mechanics Institute, he went on to study at the Art School of South Kensington,[3] again taking evening classes.

After several years of studying he said that he "now found that he could draw a bit" and much to his delight found a job as a calico designer. His designs, many of which were extremely beautiful, consisted of groups of flowers that were then reproduced for block-printing on glazed chintz. He had to conform to strict guidelines as to colour and techniques. Colours could not be blended together, and each part of the design, such as a petal or leaf, had to be drawn with an outlined edge. Commenting on his work at the calico factory a few years later, James said that his designs were of little artistic merit but, he added, "making designs gave me a certain amount of skill in arranging forms over a surface, which has no doubt helped me in my landscape work."[4]

It was during this period, when he first started at the calico factory, that James began to paint landscapes. He would go out early in the morning when most people were still asleep and draw or paint around Westminster Abbey or Kensington Gardens. He loved the outdoors and must have felt a wonderful sense of freedom as he set up his easel in the early morning or on a summer evening. In later years he took a train to Epping Forest or Croydon, where he spent many enjoyable days painting the countryside surrounding London. One of his earliest works was a series of drawings of the Cloister of Westminster Abbey.

By the early 1860s James was working only half-time at the calico factory. The cotton industry had been seriously affected by the American Civil War (1861–1865). James was, by this time, an expert floral designer as well as a fast worker and he was delighted when his employer accepted his suggestion that he reduce his hours.[5] He now had many more hours of daylight for painting. He continued to work at the calico factory until the mid 1870s.

In 1863, on 8 August, James married Amelia Wright at Bloomsbury church. They had two sons and two daughters: Frank, born 1866; Louise Nancy, born 1871; John Stacy (Jack), born 1874; and Louise, born 1881.

In the early days James relied on the annual exhibitions at the Royal Academy as a way to sell his paintings, and he submitted a few paintings every year. He did not, however, have much respect for the selection committee, who, he said, chose pictures for the exhibition for their effect rather than for any artistic merit. Walter Bayes, the artist and art critic, was of the opinion that James' work was not fully appreciated by the people who organized the exhibitions.[6] He exhibited at the Royal Academy for the first time in 1870 (*Where the Water Lilies Grow*) and continued to exhibit on a fairly regular basis until 1911, the year of his death.[7] (See Appendix I for a listing of his paintings and exhibitions.)

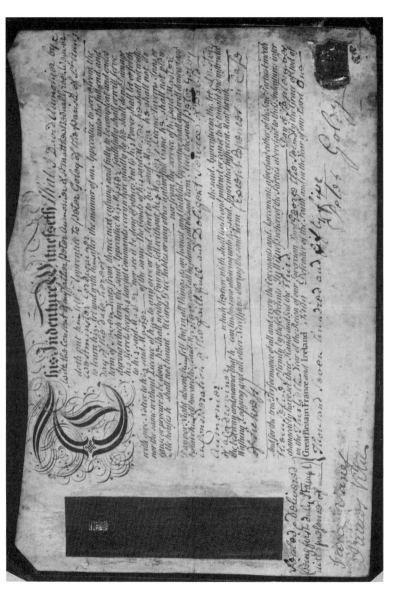

David's indenture, 1755

James as a young man

William senior, 1896

Hall seat in English oak made by William senior

In 1871 James attended Heatherley's School of Fine Art, where he not only studied art but had the opportunity to meet other painters.[8] The school had been founded in 1845 and was originally in the Art School at Maddox Street in London. It became Heatherley's in 1860, or shortly thereafter, when Thomas Heatherley became principal. It was run on the atelier system, similar to art schools in France and other European countries, and placed great importance on working from a model.[9] At Heatherley's James met the painter William Morrison Wyllie. Wyllie liked James' work, being particularly impressed with one of his landscape paintings, and he invited James to visit his studio. James accepted. Mr. Wyllie was, he said, "great with a bit of chalk and a bit of charcoal. He would say 'May I?' and then begin and chalk over my picture."[10] James appreciated the older man's advice and found that his work improved when he followed it. James soon became friends with the two Wyllie sons Charles and William Lionel who, although younger than James, were more experienced painters. Charles painted landscapes and coastal scenes, and William Lionel was a seascape painter. The Wyllie family introduced James to Lionel Smythe, the figure and landscape painter, who was a half-brother of the Wyllies and worked at the studio. These established artists gave James the encouragement and advice that he needed as he began on his career as a painter.

By the mid 1870s James may have been supporting his family by the sale of his paintings, as there are no records of any employment after he stopped working at the calico factory. He was one of many beneficiaries under the will of his cousin Henry Woollams, and he received £250.

At some point James met James Charles, the landscape and portrait painter, and the two men became firm friends. Their styles were different, but James Aumonier recognized that James Charles had some influence on his painting, and he in his turn may well have had some influence on Charles. In 1900 Charles painted a sketch portrait of Aumonier in oil.[11]

Equally skilled with watercolours and oils, James was also successful with pastels. He made sketches for paintings that he wanted to do later, rather than take photographs, as he felt that the modern technology detracted from the individuality of the finished work. He was particularly fond of late afternoon and autumn colours, the reds and golds of turning leaves, and his pictures are delicate and realistic, a sincere interpretation of natural scenes. An example of his individual style and artistic feeling is *An English Cottage Home,* which was shown at the Royal Academy in 1873 and was later bought by Sir Newton Mappin for his collection at Sheffield.

By the mid 1870s James had achieved a reputation both at home and abroad. In 1876 he was awarded the Heywood Gold Medal by the Council of the Royal Manchester Institution for his painting *Toilers in the Field.* This painting was also shown at the Royal Academy in 1876. In 1887 he received a Medal of the First Order of Merit at Melbourne, and in 1889 he received a Gold

Medal for Watercolour at the Paris International Exhibition and a Bronze Medal for Oil Painting in Adelaide. In 1878 he exhibited at L'Exposition in Paris, and in 1882 at Le Salon. He was awarded a Silver Medal at the International Exhibition in Brussels 1897, and in 1901 he exhibited in Berlin and Munich.[12]

James went abroad for the first time in 1891, when he was fifty-nine years old. He went to Italy, where he spent several months in Venice and in Belluno in the Venetian Mountains. *The River Piave, Belluno, Venetia,* and *Belluno, Venetia,* painted while he was in Italy, were exhibited at the Royal Academy in 1892 and 1893 respectively. It is interesting to note that James Charles was also in Italy in 1891, although there is no record of whether the two men were travelling companions. In 1908 James visited Spain, and his painting *A Spanish Village* is a record of this visit. In this painting he used the wet technique, moistening the paper with clear water before applying the paint, a technique that was quite popular at that time.

James became an associate of the Royal Institute of Painters in Water-Colours[13] in 1896, and he exhibited at the Institute on more than one occasion (*The Old Sussex Farmhouse* in 1895 and *The Old Chalk Pit* in 1896). In 1908 he exhibited his painting *Under the Beech Trees* at the Landscape Exhibition at the Old Watercolour Society's Galleries.[14] He exhibited at the Franco-British Exhibition in 1908 (*Evening, On a Fen Farm,* and *The School Feast*), the Japan Exhibition in 1910 (*Castle Valley, Tintagel*), the Goupil Gallery and the Leicester Galleries.[15]

James has long been thought of as a painter of English country scenes, but this is not exclusively true. His paintings from Italy and Spain, and *Gathering Bait,* painted in 1878 and later acquired by Walker Art Gallery in Liverpool, are all examples of his versatility. The latter picture shows two women on a stretch of lonely shore, searching for fishing bait in pools of water lying between slimy rocks. The sky is overcast and the overall impression is one of hardship.[16]

Over the years his work was acquired by galleries both at home and overseas. *Sheep Washing* and *Black Mountains* are part of the Chantrey Bequest Collection at the Tate Gallery, purchased in 1869 and 1905 respectively. *Sheep Washing* depicts a typical country scene in the early twentieth century with the sheep walking downstream after they have been washed by the farmhands. It is a warm summer day, the men in shirtsleeves, and children watching. The Birmingham Museum and Art Gallery purchased *A Nook in Nature's Garden* and *Sunset on the Sussex Downs.*[17] He was also represented in galleries in Capetown, Cardiff, Sheffield, Melbourne, and Adelaide.

Many new art societies were starting up at the end of the nineteenth century, and James was one of the original members of the Institute of Painters in Oil Colour. He was "hors concours" of the Paris Salon des Beaux Arts and a member of the Anglo-Australian Society of Artists, the New English Art Club, and the Society of British Pastellists.[18] Reflecting his Huguenot heritage, James was a member of the Huguenot Society.

James and Amelia moved fairly frequently. They lived in Horsey in 1870, Petersfield in 1884, Steyning in 1887, and back in London in 1888.[19] By 1896 they were living in Adelaide Road in Hampstead, where Amelia died on 23 December 1899.

A letter that James wrote to his son Frank in November 1905 provides a glimpse of a genial, warm-hearted family man. He was on holiday in Somerset with his younger son Jack, also a painter, and they stayed at Grange Farm, Buckland Saint Mary in Chard.

Dear Youngster [Frank is thirty-nine]

We are glad to hear that you are flourishing, and we also are ditto—I have got over my bad pains, and am able to knock along much as usual. We have certainly been fortunate in the weather—Sunday which Jack said "was too dark to see the paint" was with us, simply splendid, and we took a walk into Devonshire before dinner. We had two bad days last week and that is about all—it has been cold most of the time, but today has been like a genial Spring day.

I am doing some watercolour sketches to top up with—while my oil things dry—it has been very bad for drying—instead of about two or three days, it has taken a week.

I did not think much of your choice of 'halfpenny things' [postage]—two bills, and a summons to a council meeting—it seems to me that you might have managed something better than that.

Like you we have no news—at least that will interest you. "Freddy" won the first prize for boys Ploughing, at the Match on Thursday last, and also the prize for the best "turn out", and that is our only great excitement.

I fancy we shall both be glad to get back on Saturday. . . .

If you like to come down here to live, there is a good cottage with large garden that we can have for £4 a year, and about 12/– rates and taxes—what do you say to that? Perhaps Jessie [Frank's wife] would like to go in for it—she would be able to work without being much disturbed, and we know she likes that, or there is a Farm House with seven acres of ground to be sold for £400, how would that suit, if she is thinking of "settling down" perhaps she will jump at it.

Yes, you are quite right—it is all very silly, but you must make excuses for being 5 miles from everywhere—so good-bye.

With love from us both to you both, and also Jessie.

Your loving Old father J Aumonier.

James was ill during the last few months of his life and died on 4 October 1911. In the morning of that day he told his nurse that he had been "watching the sun rise since dawn."[20] He was cremated at Woking on 6 October. A memorial exhibition of his work was held at the Goupil Gallery in March 1912, and in 1924 his painting *On a Fen Farm* was included in the British Empire Exhibition.[21]

Frank was a civil servant. In 1903 he married Jessie Greasey. He died in 1949 and Jessie died in 1964.

Jack was an artist like his father, but little is known about his artistic career other than that he exhibited at the Royal Academy for several years between 1903 and 1930. His first painting to be shown there was *Carricks Road*[22] (see Appendix II for a list of his paintings shown at Royal Academy). He also worked at the Air Ministry. In 1912 Jack married Emmie Bayes; they did not have any children. He died in 1963 at the age of eighty-nine, and Emmie died in 1965.

‹ VI ›

William and the
Aumonier Studio
1839 to 1914

HENRY AND NANCY'S YOUNGEST SON William became an architectural carver and sculptor. In 1856 Nancy, who was by this time a widow, arranged for William to serve an apprenticeship with Leonard William Collmann and Joseph Davis, upholsterers, cabinet makers, and carvers, at 53 George Street, Portman Square, "to learn their art as Carver." Under the terms of the indenture, which was signed on 25 March 1856, Collmann and Davis agreed to pay William

for the first or remainder of a year the weekly sum of six shillings, for the second year (commencing the sixth day of July 1856) the weekly sum of eight shillings, for the third the weekly sum of ten shillings, and for the remaining years of the said term the weekly sum of twelve shillings.

William was seventeen years old and lived in Broad Court, Covent Garden, with James and Fred. In the evenings he took art classes at St. Martin's School of Art.

In 1858 Leonard Collmann and Joseph Davis unexpectedly terminated their partnership and went out of business. William was nineteen years old, his mother

59

had died in 1856 and he decided not to seek another apprenticeship but to work instead for established artists, in their studios. This was a fairly common practice among students in Paris at this time, but not in London.[1] William worked for a Mr. Forsythe in Hampstead Road and a Mr. Phyffers in Westminster; he then went to Paris, where he worked for a M. Cruchet, a M. Kaltenheuser, and a M. Fourdrinier,[2] again in their studios. In 1860 he moved to Amiens where he had the good fortune to meet a M. Duthoit—although it is possible that they had met before William left Paris. There were two Duthoit brothers, Aimé (1803–1869) and Louis (1807–1874), both sculptors, and a nephew, Edmond (1837–1889), who was a protégé of the architect Eugène Emmanuel Viollet-le-Duc.[3] It is not known which of the Duthoits befriended William, but it was through this friendship that William met Viollet-le-Duc and worked, under his direction, on the restoration of the cathedral in Amiens. This was a great opportunity for William, a young man starting out in life, and it had a lasting influence on his work. Viollet-le-Duc was one of the leading architects of the time and an authority on Gothic art. He designed the restoration of many medieval buildings, including the cathedrals of Amiens and Notre-Dame de Paris.

William stayed in Amiens for a year and he then went back to Paris. In 1862 he went home to London to see family and friends and to attend the International Exhibition held in London that year. He liked living in Paris and he had intended to return, but he changed his mind. Leonard Collmann was in business again, this time by himself, and he offered William a job which he accepted. And William fell in love with Anne Creasey, a petite, pretty, and energetic young woman whom everyone called Tiny.

William and Tiny were married at Marylebone Church on 24 September 1864 and had three daughters and two sons: Minnie, born 1865; Edith, born 1867; William, born 1869; Anne Louise, born 1873; and Stacy, born 1877.

Although he was gaining good experience working for Leonard Collman, William decided that he needed to broaden his outlook and in the mid to late 1860s he travelled extensively in England. Tiny and the children may have gone with him. In any event Minnie, Edith, and William were not baptized until 1870, and they were baptized together, on 17 April, at St. Mary's Church, St. Marylebone.

In the late 1860s or early 1870s William met John McKean Brydon, the architect, and a close friendship developed between the two men. John Brydon had been born in Scotland, but in the late 1860s he moved to London, where he established a decorating and furnishing business in Langham Place with two fellow architects, Wallace and Cottier.

In 1876 William, with the encouragement of John Brydon and the promise of work from Wallace and Cottier and other architects, established his own business as an architectural carver at 1 New Inn Yard, Tottenham Court Road. One of the first important carvings he executed on his own, which did much to assure his reputation, was at the London School Board offices on the Victoria Embankment. (See Appendix III for a complete listing of William's work, with the architects he worked for.) In 1876 he carved the tombstone for the grave of his cousin Henry Woollam:[4] his fee was £285. He was also a beneficiary under Henry's will and he inherited £250.

In the late 1880s William received a commission to execute the terra cotta modelling for a gable on the Victoria Law Courts in Birmingham. First he travelled to France to study this particular style of architecture and he then created the gable at a Mr. Edward's terra cotta works in Ruabon, in the county of Denbigh, Wales. He worked outdoors on a gallery placed sixty to seventy feet above the ground. This was the height of the gable on the law courts, and William worked at this height as he wanted to be able to judge the effect from the point of view of spectators, pedestrians walking in the street, who would look up to the top of the new building. There were three figures: one in the gable which represented "Art" and was about five feet high, and two below representing "Modelling" and "Designing." His design was exhibited at the Royal Academy in 1889.[5]

In the 1890s William was selected to create two carvings in St. Paul's Cathedral, the Sedilla and Fald stool and a carved panel to the front of the Bishop's Throne. The latter, with its solid inlay panel and carved border, demonstrates William's masterful use of the carver's tools. With inlay, he said, it was important to "try and get a broad effect, produced by the quality and colour of the wood itself and by the direction of the grain in which a piece of the inlay is placed . . . the occasional inaccuracies of fitting and consequent different thickness of joints give it a distinct charm of its own."[6]

In 1897 William executed carvings in the south wing of the Wordsworth Buildings at Lady Margaret Hall in Oxford. The south wing was one of several new buildings and was intended for students. Between 1905 and 1907 the architect Halsey Ricardo commissioned William to carve the timber staircase at Debenham House. Ricardo designed the house for Sir Ernest Debenham, the founder of the department store that bore his name, and he invited several of his friends from the Art Workers Guild to execute the interior designs. William is also known to have carried out some wood-carving at Chequers, the house that is now the country seat of British prime minister.[7]

For the greater part of his professional life William produced working drawings and sculptured work, mostly in stone, for architects. Occasionally he received a commission for wood-carving. Much of this work was based on historical styles. He liked to work from a full-size charcoal drawing or sketch and not clay or plaster models, which he considered to be useless and immoral in that they cost time and money which would be better spent on the carving.

Running the studio and working on commissions took up most of William's time but even so he made

time for his own work. An example of his intrinsic individuality is an oak hall seat that he carved and designed
in the late 1890s for a wedding present. It was designed
with great care. The back panel was shallow at the top
and shelved downward to a deep hollow at the bottom,
and anyone sitting on the seat could lean back with
some comfort. The only ornamentation was the carving
on the back panel, and the mouldings on the arm rests.
The carving on the back panel depicted an oak tree
and a rose tree growing from separate roots and uniting
in the middle. There was also an imaginary coat-of-
arms, which was carved and then painted.[8]

William brought intelligence and knowledge to his
craft and was a highly respected member of his profession. He accepted invitations to address the Royal Institute of British Architects on more than one occasion.[9]
He was usually among other carvers and craftsmen as
one of a panel of speakers. He gave two papers on
wood-carving, the first in 1896 and the second in 1906.
Discussing "the characteristics of true wood-carving"
(in 1896) he said:

All the beauty should be evolved out of the material itself;
being wood, it should retain the characteristics of wood, and
not made to represent marble, bronze, silver, or any other
material. Depend upon it, it is quite capable of taking care
of itself if properly treated; and by the very individuality of its
treatment it may attain a charm and beauty equal to that of
almost any substance the hand of man can fashion into art.

To this end we want it cut by a strong man, fully alive to

the capabilities and susceptibilities of his material. If he is a good workman, he will combine freshness and grace. . . . He will concentrate his mind on the firm sweep of the gouge over all, tenderly treat the thin and delicate parts which fade into the ground, and boldly undercut his projections . . . to make the work stand out free, so that it positively dances on the ground with delight.[10]

And on the second occasion (in 1906) he commented that a carving should be "alive with living, nervous cuts all over both subject and ground, making one harmonious whole . . . all parts of the work teeming with the joy of life and effort which the carver felt in doing it."[11] His words conjure up a picture of the man himself, large and vigorous, robust and cheerful, taking great delight in a beautiful piece of work.

In 1902 the Royal Institute of British Architects devoted an evening to "Inlay and Marquetry." William Aumonier and Heywood Sumner were the two speakers. William's paper was called "Veneer Work and Solid Inlay," and he discussed inlay work in wood, ivory, or shells.

William became a member of the Art Workers Guild on 9 January 1885. There is no record of the piece of work that he produced to be accepted into the guild, although a "masterpiece" was one of the requirements of membership, or became so. He was one of the original members. The guild was founded in 1884 by Walter Crane and Lewis Day with the purpose of encouraging artists and craftsmen to develop and maintain the highest standards of artistry. The sculptor George Blackall-Simonds was the first Master.[12]

The Guild held its first "Revels" in 1900. Supper was provided, and there was punch to drink. However, the punch was not as innocuous as it tasted, and before long the quietest members became very talkative. William was his usual exuberant self. He played his drum—he may have been part of the entertainment put on by some of the members—and he thoroughly enjoyed himself. At the end of the evening he began to make his noisy way homeward, but had not gone far before he was cautioned by a policeman to go home quietly. William wanted to show the policeman his talent for drum-playing, but the officer was having none of this. He found out William's address, hailed a cab and sent him on his way.[13]

Like many artists William had his own style of dressing. The guild members caused quite a stir in the quiet village of Penshurst in Kent when they held one of their meetings there. William wore a large sombrero and a wide royal blue cummerbund, while some of the other members wore flannels and straw hats.[14]

In the 1890s William and Tiny lived near Camden Square, and by 1903 they were living at 40 Lambolle Road in Hampstead. In November 1903 William was elected a Fellow of the Huguenot Society.

During the last two years of his life illness forced William into retirement and prevented him from attending the meetings at the Art Workers Guild, which he had always enjoyed. He died at his home in Hampstead on

21 January 1914. He was seventy-four and a half years old. He was well-known in his field, and the reputation that he had deservedly earned for the Aumonier studio was continued into the next two generations by his son William and his grandson Eric.

Tiny died in 1929, at the age of ninety-four, without knowing that Stacy, her younger son, had died the previous December. She became very forgetful during the last few months of her life and, as Stacy had been living in Switzerland, the family decided not to tell her of his death. A photograph of Tiny which was taken during her later years and bore a remarkable resemblance to a Whistler portrait, was, according to her obituary, displayed in many Underground stations during the late 1920s.

William and Tiny's elder son William followed in his father's footsteps and became an architectural carver and sculptor, while Stacy became a writer, as we shall see in Chapters VII and VIII.

‹ ✳ ›

Neither Minnie nor Edith, the two older daughters, married. Minnie was a watercolour artist and a poet, and her paintings of gardens, flowers, and birds had a charm that appealed to many people. Her painting *Lilies and Lavender* was exhibited at the Royal Academy in 1920.[15] Her poetry was rather sentimental, but sincere: in the late 1920s she published *The Poetry of Gardens in Watercolours and Verse*, a slim volume of twelve short poems and six paintings, which she called coloured drawings. She also produced Christmas and greeting cards.

Minnie and Edith lived in Golders Green next door to their sister Annie, who was an actress. Annie married Harry Farmer, and they had four children. Minnie and Annie died in 1952 and Edith died in 1953.

‹ VII ›

Stacy

1877 to 1928

STACY PURSUED at least three different careers in the arts over the course of his short lifetime. His métier, though, was writing and it was as a writer of short stories that he earned his reputation.

When he was thirteen years old his father sent him to Cranleigh, a boarding school for boys. Stacy attended the school for three years, from the beginning of the Michaelmas (Autumn) Term 1890 to the end of the Summer Term 1893. He belonged to the Literary and Debating Society and was a full prefect during his last term. Stacy kept in touch with his old school and in 1901 designed a new cover for the school magazine, *The Cranleighan.* It was used for the first time on the April 1901 issue, which was, as the editor noted in the introduction, the first edition of the new century. He credited Stacy with the design and he also commented that Stacy Aumonier's name was proof, if it was needed, of its artistic merit.[1]

Stacy studied decorative design when he left school and probably pursued a career in this field for several years. In 1908 he was described as an architect in the catalogue of the Royal Academy when he exhibited a design for the entrance hall of a house ("Walden," in West Horsely).[2]

In 1907 Stacy married Gertrude Peppercorn, a concert pianist, and in 1908 he began his second career, that of a performing artist or "society entertainer," as he was called. He wrote character sketches that he performed, as a solo performer, at several theatres in London including the Comedy and the Criterion. His impersonations were unselfconscious and true to life and he was able to portray a variety of characters with equal success. Among the parts he played were a garrulous "Old Woman in a Shawl," "The Compleat Englishman" and "Otto of Stuttgart."[3]

Stacy enjoyed painting and he evidently had some talent. Two of his paintings were selected for exhibit at the Royal Academy: *On the Downs, Sussex* (1902) and *Buildings by the Zuyder Zee* (1903). In 1911 an exhibition of his work was held at the Goupil Gallery. He also exhibited at the Royal Institute.[4]

By 1913 he was beginning to establish himself as a writer, and in 1917 he had two books published: *The Friends and Other Stories* and a novel, *Three Bars Interval. The Friends* was the first of Stacy's stories to attract literary attention. The friends in this story are two men, both furniture salesmen, whose common bond is drinking. It is a story of boredom, despair, and loneliness, and the two friends eventually drink themselves to death. His agent did not like the story and rejected it. Stacy then made his own arrangements, and *The Friends* was published in the *English Review* in London and the

Century Magazine in New York. Subsequently, the readers of *Transcript*, a magazine published in Boston, voted it one of fifteen best stories of the year. John Galsworthy described it as one of Stacy's most powerful stories. *Miss Bracegirdle and Others* (1923) is one of his better known collections of crime stories.[5] (See Appendix IV for a complete list of his publications.)

Stacy was thirty-seven years old when World War I broke out in 1914. He served first as a private in the Army Pay Corps and later worked at the Ministry of National Service making charts. His novel *The Querrils,* which was about a family living in London during the war, was published in 1919. Many people found that they could identify with the kind-hearted family portrayed in the book who continually ignored the deprivations and suffering that occurred as a result of the war. It was well received and proved to be a popular book.

Stacy's novels and short stories reflect the charm and humour of an interesting and interested person. In his writing he gave his imagination full rein but even so was able to create stories that were realistic and credible. Rebecca West in her review of his novel *Heartbeat* (1922) praised his ability to blend reality with the imaginary: an attribute, she wrote, that was the "the envy of all artists." John Galsworthy admired Stacy's story-telling skills, his ability to hold the reader's interest from the first word to the last. But Stacy did not always receive good reviews. Kathleen Mansfield, writing in the *Athenaeum,* described his novel *One After Another* (1922) as dull and uninteresting. Some people liked his stories because they were easy to read, others thought that this made them appear glib and mechanical.[6]

Stacy was an attractive man with piercing eyes and wavy hair tumbling over his forehead. He always wore a black stock, a form of necktie that was particularly popular among artists in the early twentieth century.[7] Warm-hearted and congenial, he was a charming companion and had many friends who enjoyed his company and his sense of humour. He was a member of the Savage and Pen Clubs.

In 1926 Stacy and Gertrude went on holiday to Dorset. While he was away Stacy wrote to John Galsworthy. There is no record of the year that the two men met, but they appear to have been on friendly terms. Stacy's letter was in response to a letter from Galsworthy, who had written to Stacy telling him that he had enjoyed his story *The Baby Grand*. Stacy wrote of his happiness at receiving Galsworthy's kind remarks and how much he, in his turn, had enjoyed *The Silver Spoon*. He continued with comments about the character of Soames in *The Forsyte Saga*. In 1929 Galsworthy wrote the foreword to *Ups and Downs*, a collection of Stacy's short stories which was published after his death.[8]

Stacy and Gertrude had one son, Timothy, born 1921, and by the mid 1920s they were all living in Ewell in Surrey. At about this time Stacy contracted tuberculosis, and his health began to fail. From August to December 1927 he was a patient at Selbrigg Sanitarium in Norfolk, which was run by Dr. and Mrs. Morris. The patients lived in huts that were cold and damp, especially in the winter, but Dr. Morris assured Stacy that this was not harmful to the patients.[9] In October he was a little better and had gained weight, but by November he was in bed again and could only speak in a whisper. His brother Willie went to see him in November. It was a cold wet weekend but he found Stacy in a good humour, optimistic and expecting to recover. By the end of December he was well enough to go home.[10]

There is correspondence from Stacy to Rebecca West from this period. His letters are warm and friendly. Miss West invited Stacy and Gertrude for a visit, but Stacy had to decline because of his health. He indicated, though, that Gertrude would enjoy such a visit.[11]

Stacy and Gertrude decided to spend the winter of 1928–9 in Switzerland. They hoped that the mountain air would be good for Stacy. In August Gertrude had gone to Switzerland for a few days and rented an apartment in Montana, in the Valais. Stacy never returned home, dying in Montana on 24 December 1928 at the age of fifty-one. He was sustained by his faith and belief in God during the long months of his illness. He thought of God as a friend and did not fear death.

Stacy did not leave a will, and his estate at the time of his death was valued for probate at £1,000.[12] Gertrude died in 1966.

Timothy, their son, had a wife named Maureen and five children: Phillip Stacy, Clare, Andrew, John, and Patrick.

‹ VIII ›

84 Charlotte Street

WILLIAM AND TINY'S ELDEST SON William was a craftsman and artist who, like his father, became a successful sculptor and carver. On 11 July 1905 William junior, or Willie, as he was frequently called, became a partner in the family business, and the Aumonier Studio was renamed Aumonier and Son. Willie was twenty-five years old.

Unfortunately, little is known about Willie's education and training. In 1893 he went to the United States for about a year and worked as a modeller, first in New York City and then in Glens Falls, a small town on Lake George in New York State, where, he said, the only relaxation was the Quaker Meeting House on Sundays. This must have been quite a change of pace for young William, who was used to the artistic and cosmopolitan life of London. He revisited Glens Falls briefly in 1903.

Willie always liked to travel, and in 1889 he went to Paris for the first time, to go to the World's Fair. He went with a friend: the two young men had about £7 each to spend, and they stayed until it was gone. Although he revisited the city many times, he said "I don't think I ever recaptured the glamour of that first visit." Over the years he visited Norway, Denmark, Sweden, France, Italy, Austria, Germany, Switzerland, the Netherlands, the United States, and Canada.

In 1895, when he was twenty-six years old, Willie married Julia Florence Allison, the daughter of George Allison and Julia Augusta Whitworth. Julia Florence was two years older than Willie. She was the sixth of eight children, a family of five girls and three boys. Her father had been born in Berwick-on-Tweed, and as a young man he had moved to London where he became a civil servant working at Somerset House. The Allisons lived comfortably in London Fields, just south of Hackney. George went into the city every day on horseback, followed by a groom on a second horse. The groom later returned home with both horses, and in the evening they followed the same procedure, in reverse. George died in 1873 at the age of forty-three. He had managed his affairs well, and the family was far from destitute; even so, his widow decided to move to a smaller house, in Finchley, maybe on the advice of her stepbrother Henry Gutierrez, who took care of her affairs after the death of George. Unfortunately he made a poor investment—whether he lacked good judgment or suffered bad luck is not clear—putting most of her capital, as well as his own, in to the new electric lighting. They both lost a great deal of money. Julia Augusta decided to stay in the house at Finchley but was forced to let out part of it. The family was split up and Julia Florence went to live with her mother's half-sister Wynanda,[1] who was married to James Havill. Aunt Havill, as she was called, was a warmhearted and kind woman, and she treated Julia Florence like her own daughter, providing for her and educating her. It was she who introduced Julia to Willie.

Soon after they were married, Willie and Julia moved to Northwood, just outside London. Julia was very happy to be living in the country again; they kept chickens, and their house, "The Sagamore," had a large garden. Their four children were all born in Northwood: Whitworth in 1896, Eric in 1899, Pierre in 1903, and Mary in 1907. When Mary was born Willie wrote:

> A soft still night
> When all the world's asleep
> One star above
> To herald to the Angels
> The first flower of Spring is born.

Willie was working very hard. He spent long days at the studio and taught evening classes in modelling and carving at Art Schools in Battersea, Camberwell, and Blackheath—all a long way from Northwood. At the end of the evening he took the horse-drawn omnibus to Baker Street and then a slow steam train to Northwood. Not only did he find the travelling very tiresome, but he had less and less time to spend with Julia and the children, so in 1908 or 1909 they moved back to London. They bought a large comfortable house in Brondesbury. There was a garden in the back that Julia loved, and Willie was happy to "dig myself into dear old London once more."

As his father's health began to fail, Willie gradually

Stacy

William junior, Whitworth, Julia, Tiny, and Michael, 1924

The keystones at York House carved by William junior

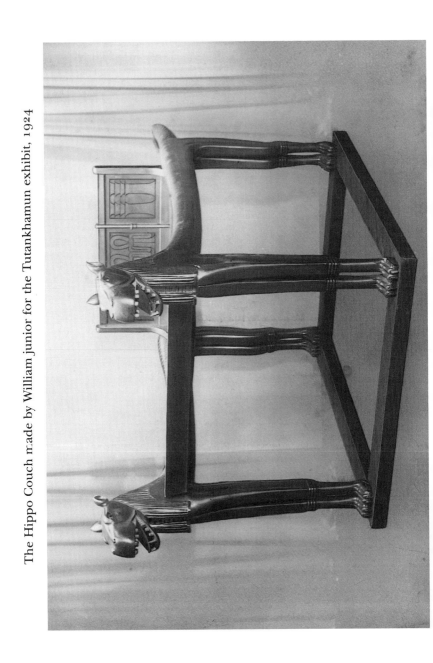

The Hippo Couch made by William junior for the Tutankhamun exhibit, 1924

took over the management of Aumonier and Sons. Over the years he expanded production while maintaining the reputation his father had earned before him and that he then earned for himself. Under his guidance the studio produced exquisite objects of art, interesting pieces with charm and character, and visitors entering the studio experienced a sense of richness and beauty. There were pieces in metal and marble, in beautiful fine-grained and coloured woods; there were carvings in ivory, wood, marble, and stone, and Willie used colour—including gold, silver, and bronze—as it had been used in Greek temples and later in English churches, to enhance the sculpture, and not just to create a pattern.[2]

Willie produced work for many of the leading architects in London, as indeed his father had done. The first big contract that he carried out on his own was at the Hong Kong and Shanghai Bank in Gracechurch Street for W. Campbell, Jones, Son and Smithers. In 1926 he produced the keystones on York House for the architects Whinney, Son and Austen Hall. York House was built as a showpiece for the Gas Light and Coke Company and the keystones are examples of some of Willie's finest stonework demonstrating his individuality and craftsmanship. (See Appendix V for a listing of William's work and his architects.)

Willie executed carvings at Australia House in Westminster, both inside and out. The carvings on the outside, two figures over the entrance, attracted a considerable amount of attention. In his paper *Huguenot*

London (1923), W. H. Manchee remarked that it was appropriate that these particular carvings had been executed by William, who was of Huguenot descent.[3] The early Huguenot refugees had settled in Westminster, and Pierre II (as was noted in Chapter I) had been a member of the Church of the Tabernacle, Glasshouse Street, Leicester Fields.

Working from charcoal drawings, Willie carved directly on to the stone of a building. "The stone carver," he wrote "is the architect's greatest ally, for it is the stone-carving that will make or mar a building. . . . Architecture and stone-carving are so intimately related that one cannot fail without injuring the other."[4] He frequently worked from scaffolding, exposed to all weathers and perched high above the ground. He was conscientious: before he executed the stone carving on the Westminster Bank, Angel Court, Lothbury, he went to Italy to study and obtain at first hand the details he needed for this work.[5]

After World War I Willie received numerous commissions to design and produce war memorials (he claimed that he was associated with ninety). The Menin Gate at Ypres was probably one of his greatest achievements. Willie would not have agreed: all memorials, he said, told the story of sacrifice and one was no more important or significant than another. The Alfreton War Memorial, Derbyshire, which he designed and carved, was described as beautifully artistic in symmetry, solidarity, and gracefulness of general outline. It consisted of a two-step platform of hard York stone, surrounded by pillars and kerbs of Cornish granite, surmounted by massive bronze standards and bronze chain connections. The square panelled base and pedestal were constructed from Portland stone. On the north side of the pedestal there was an inscription and the names of the one hundred and sixteen men of Alfreton who gave their lives for their country. The statue, in bronze, is a realistic representation of a British soldier in full service gear. Standing at ease with his rifle at rest in his left hand, his right arm is placed protectively around the figure of a child, who symbolizes the rising and future generation for whom the supreme sacrifice was made.[6] This memorial was an example of Willie's philosophy that there were vast and boundless opportunities at hand for the carver to express his individuality with power and beauty. In this postwar period the studio also produced models of regimental cap badges to be used in a cemetery in France where hundreds of British men were buried.

By the mid 1920s Willie's two sons, Whitworth and Eric, were also working at the studio. The business continued to grow and by 1928 Willie employed twenty-five craftsmen who were expert in clay, plaster, wood, and stone.

In 1923 Willie received a commission to produce a replica of Tutankhamun's Tomb for the British Empire Exhibition, which was to be held in the north-west London suburb of Wembley that year. Tutankhamun's Tomb had been discovered at Luxor in 1922 and was very much in the news at the time. The commission came about in a strange way. The Architectural Association had invited Willie to address students of a modelling class and to judge their work. The following day one of the students from the class came to see Willie. A friend had asked him to make a small model of Tutankhamun's Tomb and, although the friend had provided details, he was running into difficulties. Would Mr. Aumonier help? Willie agreed, although he considered the fee completely inadequate.

This chance encounter led to Willie's acquaintance with Arthur Weigall, the Egyptologist, and finally to the important commission to reproduce the contents of four chambers of the tomb for the Wembley Exhibition. Mr. Weigall provided Willie with photographs and sketches of the tomb and gave advice and help whenever it was needed. It took twelve craftsmen, including Whitworth and Eric, eight months to complete the work. Chairs of ivory and ebony, fearsome elongated cows and lions, golden chariots and chests, armed black slaves, and the Pharaoh's chair were all included in this vast production. The fine gold used to gild the lions and chariots cost over a thousand pounds. The exhibit was displayed in a small building on the periphery of the amusement park at the British Empire Exhibition.[7]

Howard Carter, the archaeologist who discovered the tomb, felt that the Tutankhamun exhibits in Wembley were an infringement of his rights. He assumed that the pieces had been created with the aid of copyrighted photographs and a writ was taken out against the Directors of the British Empire Exhibition. Willie and Arthur

Weigall were able to prove that they did not use Carter's photographs and the case was dismissed.

When the exhibition closed Willie bought back most of the pieces and set them up permanently at 84 Charlotte Street. In an attempt to create the right atmosphere, he put them in a windowless basement room with one small light over the doorway.[8]

This important commission sealed Willie's reputation and that of the studio and led to further commissions for display work. For several years the studio produced a series of rooms for the Daily Mail Ideal Home Exhibition and in 1925 Willie was invited to participate in Selfridges' sixteenth birthday celebration. For the latter the studio produced a large display of decorative sculptures, including torch-bearers and figures symbolizing the arts, commerce, and travel. Also in 1925, the studio received a silver medal of the first class for the colour decorations in the British Pavilion at the Paris Exhibition of International Decorative Art.

In 1925 Willie produced *The Song of the Chisel*, a small book for private circulation. In the dedication to his grandson Michael he wrote: "This little record of my life's work has no pretension to any importance, it merely records a page in the architectural history of this generation." It was, however, a photographic record of the sculptural work and carving produced at the Aumonier studio over the years and included pieces by his father and by Eric. In 1929 Willie published part of his collection of photographs of modern decorative carving in a book entitled *Modern Architectural Sculpture*. It included all styles ranging from orthodox to ultramodern and represented works from many countries including Great Britain, the United States, Canada, Norway, Sweden, Denmark, Holland, France, Germany, Spain, and Italy. In an article in the *Architectural Review* (October 1929) Willie is credited with being one of the first people to publish a collection of work produced by modern architectural carvers.

Willie was elected to membership of the Art Workers Guild on 6 February 1914.[9] He was president of the Master Carvers Association for three years and he was also a member of many other art clubs and associations, including the Architectural Association and the Design and Industries Association.[10]

Willie had many interests. He was a member of the Huguenot Society, he enjoyed writing poetry, he owned a movie camera and projector and made family movies, and he was an enthusiastic family historian.

His uncle Fred shared his interest in family history and the two men corresponded regularly, exchanging facts and information. Willie attempted to make contact with the French branch of the family but met with little success. In the late 1920s he corresponded with a Pasteur D. Bourchenin who had been born in Lezay in Poitou and was connected, through marriage, to the Aumonier family living in that area;[11] but a connection between them and Pierre I could not be established.

‹ IX ›

Family Life

Willie and Julia

WILLIE AND JULIA moved to Fordwych Road in Brondesbury, in north-west London, in 1908 or 1909. Their house, number 93, and garden were large, ideal for raising a family. Life at home was pleasant and contented. Willie and Julia were happily married; they were affectionate and caring parents and they were "blessed with loving and beautifully minded children."[1]

A large number of relatives lived in north-west London. Grandpa and Granny Aumonier (William and Tiny) lived in Hampstead—William died in 1914—and Minnie and Edith, Willie's two unmarried sisters, lived in Golders Green next door to the youngest sister Annie and her husband Harry Farmer and their four children. Two of Julia's sisters, Maggie and Ethel, and two of her brothers, George and Cuthbert, all lived in London. Maggie did not marry and at one time she lived with Julia and Willie. George was married to Sarah (Auntie Tots) and they had four children; and Ethel was married to William Payne, a doctor, and they had two children.

Whitworth was eighteen in 1914, at the beginning of

83

World War I, and he enlisted in the Royal Army Medical Corps as a private. Eric, who was a frail child and was said to have had a "weak heart," was fifteen years old, Pierre was eleven, and Mary was seven. Pierre was a happy little boy and in 1928 Julia wrote to him about the war years:

My dear I always feel whatever I endured during the war, you and I shared it together very closely. You knew and saw how I worked and all I use to do . . . without your dear loving ways and help I could not have carried on . . . your dear happy face and happy ways gave me such courage. Directly you got home from school, I used to feel, thats all right Pierres home.[2]

In 1918 Whitworth was stationed in Jaffa, and a few months before the war ended he went on leave to Cairo. He was observant, with a keen sense of humour, and he wrote about this experience to his family:

On Wednesday morning, March 6, 1918, I drew £8, or rather 780 Piastres, in notes etc., and these I put away in my pay book next to my heart! After an early dinner we left our billets in Jaffa on a wagon and proceeded to the Railhead. . . . We found a train . . . with its head towards Kantara, so we got on board. It was a bit dark. . . . it was a truck of some sort without a roof, but it had a floor so we were satisfied. We made the distressing discovery at the end of the journey that our truck had brought coal up!!

It took seventeen hours to reach Kantara, and by the time they arrived "we all looked like sweeps." They changed trains in Kantara and arrived in Cairo at 5 o'clock in the afternoon. He continued:

84

No sooner had we got out of the station than we were surrounded by guides, hotel proprietors, natives selling walking
sticks and other articles and more guides. . . . One of the
guides stuck to us; he said he was from the Y.M.C.A. Corner
House, and as that was where we intended to stay, we followed him. He got us a "Garry," or cab, and we drove
through the streets of Cairo. We booked our room, or rather
beds, as we slept on camp bedsteads on the landing the first
night. . . . What a treat it was to be in a bed! with sheets too!
for the first time for over two and a half years!

He visited the bazaars, mosques, shops, and museums
but found the guides "a terrible nuisance, worse than
mosquitoes!"

Pierre was a restless young man. He wanted to travel
and see the world, and in 1921, when he was eighteen
years old, he went to New Zealand and worked on a
sheep farm for a year. By the end of 1922 he was back
in London and then in 1924 he set off again, this time
for Canada. He had intended to go on to New Zealand,
but he settled in Canada and by 1928 he was living in
Calgary. Finding a job was not easy. Notices advertising
employment frequently included the phrase "no English need apply." There were many Central Europeans,
who spoke little or no English and were willing to take
half wages, also looking for work. Pierre was adaptable
and quickly adjusted to the conditions and circum-
stances of the life he had chosen. Julia and Willie wor-
ried about him: "We are so far away that we are always
so anxious for you to get settled in to some thing good
with some future in it."[3]

She sent him money:

Now dear I will enclose 1£ in this and one in my next letter and one in the first week in November making 3£ altogether and I will tell you what I want you to do with it, portion it out 5/– a week for *extra* food for the winter.[4]

Julia and Pierre wrote to each other frequently and her letters are a record of family events in the late 1920s.

Whitworth and Eric both became carvers and sculptors and by the mid 1920s they were working at the studio. Whitworth was the first of the four children to get married. In 1923 he married Dorothy Emmeline Clarice Lees, an Australian, and they lived in Wembley Park in north-west London. They had two children: Michael, born 1924, and Elisabeth Anne, born 1925.

Eric and Mary lived at home. They enjoyed each other's company and sometimes, on a Saturday evening, would go together to a local dance in nearby Golders Green.[5] This was an era of dinner dances and tea dances, and Mary was pretty and good company and had many friends.

In 1925 Mary met Dennis Pilcher. Dennis lived in Brighton, where he was articled to a chartered surveyor, and he met Mary in 1925 when he went to London to take exams. He stayed with a friend of his parents, Mrs. Frisby, who also knew the Aumoniers, and it was her daughter Margaret (or Frissy as everyone called her) who introduced the young pair to each other. Dennis was the oldest son of Charlie and Irene Pilcher, who lived in Hampshire. By the end of May Mary had "'turned down' all her admirers except Frissy's friend." Willie, however was "not very keen on the friendship."[6] This was hard on Julia, who wanted to support her husband but did not want to stand in the way of her daughter's happiness.

The spring of 1926 was altogether a difficult time for Willie. It was cold and wet, he did not feel particularly well, and he had many business worries as a result of the General Strike in May when all his men downed tools.

Eric, Dennis, and Mary all worked as volunteers during the strike: Eric and Dennis in the Special Constabulary, and Mary at the recruiting office for bus drivers. Whitworth volunteered to work on the railway, but by the time he applied they had enough men. Julia wrote to Pierre:

a little rioting goes on now and then in the High Road and The Crown [a pub whose forecourt was used as a bus terminal] where the buses and trams start. The other side of London is most serious from what we hear. Eric . . . with the car is out all day and night if needed, he took a car load of police late Saturday to a mob and several arrests were made. He left home 5.30 this morning and its now tea time and he's not been home, he wants real excitement where he can use his truncheon. Each bus has a bus driver (such swells) beside him a special constable and a police man, they are wired in because of stone throwing and the bonnet of the bus is covered in barbed wire and some times the windows are wired over, its exciting times these days. Most railways are working very well by volunteer's service, Whitworth applied but they have enough men. . . . I am not able to send any papers until after the Strike, nothing over 8oz no parcels. . . . The Strike is so like war times it makes everyone so friendly so ready to help each other. We get funny little news papers.[7]

At the end of May, soon after the strike ended, Willie decided he needed a holiday. Leaving Whitworth and Eric to manage the studio, he went on a two-week boat trip by himself to the Canary Islands. It was not only quiet at home without him but "it seems so funny, we have not been able to hear a word from him since he started."[8]

In September Mary went to Brussels for three months to study art and French. She was nineteen years old and Julia and Willie did not want her to travel by herself. Willie went with her and they arrived in Brussels on 12 September, a Sunday, and Willie left on the Tuesday. This was the first time Mary had lived away from home and she was homesick and miserable. She counted the days until December when she was to go home. She studied art at the Academy, taking classes every day except Sunday, had private French lessons, and also took dressmaking classes. Her father had friends in Brussels who entertained her, taking her to the theatre and the opera. Willie went to visit her in October, bringing one of her aunts with him. They went to Ypres, to see the Menin Gate which Willie had carved, and to Bruges.

After she returned to London Mary worked for Debenham & Freebody as a fashion artist. She produced drawings for the store catalogues and local newspapers.

Julia enjoyed visiting family and friends. She liked to spend the afternoon in Wembley with Dorothy and the children or go and see Tiny, Willie's mother. Tiny was "a wonderful old lady"—she died in 1929 at the age of ninety-four: "[she] always asks after you and everyone —then she forgets and asks again. I am sure she asked me thirty times how is Mary and what is she doing. Of course poor darling she is a bit trying."[9]

There was always a big family party at Christmas. Eric, Mary, Whitworth and Dorothy, Elisabeth Anne and Michael, Julia's sister Maggie, and Willie's two sisters Minnie and Edith would all be there joining in the festivities. When Whitworth, Eric, Pierre, and Mary were children it would be the occasion for a family performance. The children would dress up in costumes, usually made by Julia, and sing, dance, or recite a poem.

Minnie and Edith spent the winter of 1927–8 on the Isle of Wight. On the last Monday in November, a few days before they left, Julia and Willie invited them to lunch and "gave them a little Christmas dinner, turkey etc. and then Auntie Tots and Eileen [her daughter] came to tea so we've had a busy day, but a very happy chatty one." The sort of day that Julia enjoyed. Earlier in the month Michael spent the night with his grandparents and they took him to see the toys at Selfridges.[10]

Willie was an active member of the Art Workers Guild and he took part in the Revels in February 1928. Julia went to the performance, which she said was excellent.[11]

Willie and Julia gave a dance at a local hotel to cele-

brate Mary's twenty-first birthday in February 1928.
There were over 115 guests, and some of Mary's
friends, who were students at the Architectural Association, came in costume. It was a very successful, happy
party: "Everyone writes it was the jolliest dance they
have even been to." Julia had remarkable energy, "we
got home about 4 in the morning and on the Sunday,
no end of people came over to supper, it was so jolly."
Dennis and Mary became engaged in July 1928. Willie,
it seems, had developed warmer feelings for his future
son-in-law. "We are delighted," Julia wrote to Pierre,
"he is such a splendid boy with a fine character and
devoted to Mary and a splendid future and his parents
are awfully nice, also grandparents . . . and they have all
loved Mary from the very first."[12]

Julia must have felt a sense of relief as well as happiness that her only daughter's future was secure. She became ill early in 1928 and the doctors diagnosed cancer
of the stomach—she never knew this and always
thought she had an ulcer. She had two operations and
was very disappointed when the second one was unsuc-
cessful. By July she was in bed most of the time, and she
moved from the hot and noisy bedroom at the front of
the house, which she and Willie had always shared, into
the old nursery at the back. Cool and quiet, this was a
pretty room that had recently been repainted mauve
and blue with green cupboards. Her bed was near the
window, and she was able to look out at the little rock
garden and the crazy-paving path.[13] She died in her
sleep on 29 September 1928 and was buried a few days

later at Golders Green Cemetery. It was a beautiful sunny day, and "there were over 50 most gorgeous wreaths from various friends."[14]

‹ ✳ ›

In 1930 Willie went on a long and successful tour of Canada and the United States, which he described as a "triumphal procession." He started off in good style. On 26 July he sailed from Southampton to Montreal on the Cunard liner *Ausonia*. A Montreal newspaper reported his arrival: "Among the important passengers ... was W. Aumonier, British sculptor."[15] His reputation preceded him. *Modern Architectural Sculpture* had recently been published, and he had just completed three years as president of the Master Carvers Association. He enjoyed discussing local architecture and was flattered when his opinion was sought.

Willie travelled across Canada by train and car to Calgary, to visit Pierre and his new wife, Marion Hansen. They had married in 1929, shortly after Pierre began working for the Canadian Pacific Railway.

By mid-September Willie was in the United States. He is known to have visited Philadelphia, Baltimore, and New York. In Philadelphia he stayed with Mr. and Mrs. Hopkinson-Evans in Radnor; he was the guest of honour at a luncheon at the Art Club given by Frank Hopkinson-Evans and attended by many of the city's architects. While he was in Baltimore he visited the sculptor Louis Rosenthal at his studio in North Charles Street, and on Thursday, 6 November 1930, he was guest of honour at a luncheon given by "The Friends of the Art." Willie was a good speaker, he was well liked, and people enjoyed his company.

At the end of his tour he visited New York. Some of his thoughts about architecture and sculpture in New York and other cities in the eastern United States were printed in the New York *World.* He was fascinated with skyscrapers, although he did not particularly like their shape and he suggested that American architects sometimes needed the guiding hand of a sculptor. He cited the Chrysler Building as an example of contemporary architecture that was decorative and modern.[16] Willie returned home at the end of November.

Willie did not consider himself an academic man, but he was well informed and knowledgeable and was frequently invited to give lectures. In March 1933 he gave a lecture on ultra-modern sculpture at the Institute of the Incorporated Association of Architects and Surveyors, and during the course of the evening he showed slides of the work of Ivan Mestrovic. A member of the audience, the sculptor Sir Alfred Gilbert, interrupted the lecture several times and finally walked out in protest. Willie, however, took this in his stride and emphasized that, while everyone might not like the work, it was by a well-known German sculptor and should be taken seriously. Many people did not understand or like the new styles in art and architecture, but Willie did, and his comments were invariably balanced and wise. He had a much more receptive audience when he repeated the lecture a few nights later for the West Riding Society of Architecture in Yorkshire.[17]

Later in the same month, March 1933, he gave a lecture on modern art at Bristol University. The following day he toured the Central Employment Exchange. This was a newly constructed building and was, Willie said, an example of the alliance between art and industry; he also noted that money had not been wasted on unnecessary decoration. When he asked about the possibility of a hold-up at the Exchange, he was told that the police station was across the road, and that the money was quite safe as it was kept in a series of spring-locked drawers. In the event of an emergency the clerk had only to close the drawer and it would lock automatically and could not be opened without a master key.[18]

By the mid 1930s business had begun to decline at the Aumonier Studio. Architectural carving was one of the first of the decorative arts to be affected by world and national events and the studio was sold in the mid or late 1930s.

Willie insisted on living by himself in the big old house in Fordwych Road. His last years were lonely and sad. He wrote, "The sun no longer shines on the milestones [of life]. They grow dim and painful to read." Whitworth and Eric visited him frequently, and Elisabeth Anne and Michael often spent the night with their grandfather. The air-raids during the war did not bother him and he slept through them. His two sisters Minnie and Edith lived in a "constant state of alarm" but, he wrote to Pierre, "if one's going to be bombed one might just as well be in bed as anywhere else, and when one is turned 70, what does it matter anyway!"[19]

Willie died in December 1943. He was seventy-six years old.

< X >

Whitworth, Eric, Pierre, and Mary

BY 1931 WHITWORTH AND ERIC were running the studio, but they were never named as partners. Whitworth had a good sense of business, and Eric, who was the most creative of Willie and Julia's four children, "a worthy successor"[1] to his father and grandfather, was responsible for artistic production.

Whitworth's training as a carver was delayed until after the 1914–18 war, and he then served an apprenticeship in his father's studio. He executed carvings on several war memorials, and in 1924 he worked with Eric and Willie on the reconstruction of Tutankhamun's Tomb for the British Empire Exhibition. Unfortunately there are no other records of his work, except for an oak scroll that he carved to gain admission to the Art Workers Guild. He became a member of the guild on 5 February 1932.[2] He was also a member of the Master Carvers Association.

Management of the day-to-day activities at 84 Charlotte Street took up a considerable amount of Whitworth's time, but even so he continued to work as a wood-carver until the studio closed in the late 1930s.

Whitworth and his father were both in touch with

95

the Liverpool branch of the family. In 1929 they met Charles, the great-grandson of David who had settled in Liverpool, when he visited London. This appears to have been the only meeting, although Whitworth and Charles corresponded fairly regularly for many years. They had a common interest—the history of the Aumonier family. In keeping with his interests and family tradition Whitworth was a member of the Huguenot Society.

Whitworth had many talents. In the late 1920s he compiled and edited a family journal, *The Wheels of Time*. It lapsed after a few years and was revived in the early 1980s by his daughter, Elisabeth Anne.

Dorothy died in 1937. Whitworth, Michael, and Elisabeth Anne stayed in London during the war and Whitworth worked for the Special Police Force. In the early 1960s he moved to Sussex and in 1961 he married Winifred Burke. Whitworth died in 1975 and Winifred in 1997.

Michael, Whitworth and Dorothy's son, became an engineer and eventually settled in Belfast. He married Betty Jarvis and they had two sons, William and Jonathan. Michael died in 1974 and Betty in 1993.

Elisabeth Anne emigrated to Canada in the late 1940s. She lives in Ontario with her husband Bert Hopkins. They had three children: Janine, born 1956; Heather, born 1962; and Neil, who was born in 1958 and died in an accident in 1984.

‹ * ›

There are no records of Eric's apprenticeship or train-ing, although it is known that he studied at the Slade School of Art. According to the writer and art critic Kineton Parkes he was primarily a modeller, but he was also a highly talented sculptor and carver with a mod-ern, individual style that was neither classical nor con-ventional. He did not, however, receive the recognition and acclaim that his work merited.

In 1929 Eric was one of six sculptors commissioned to carve *The Temple of the Winds* on the new headquarters of the London Underground at St. James's Park Sta-tion. The other five sculptors were Allan Wyon, Eric Gill, A. H. Gerard, F. Rabinovitch, and Henry Moore.[3] Working directly on the stone exterior of the building, these six men created their pieces with the simplest tools, chipping and hacking, as carvers have done since the thirteenth century. Each carving was about eight feet long and entirely the work of its creator. The *Tem-ple,* "a structure as clear as the winds themselves,"[4] con-veyed an impression of movement and speed and gave meaning to the building, the headquarters of the Lon-don Underground. Eric's figure, *South Wind,* on the west side of the north wing, cannot be seen from the street. It was well designed and carved and was consid-ered to be the most architectural of all the figures and therefore the most successful. It is a strong piece. The right arm is bent back at the elbow, and the left arm is stretched horizontally backwards towards the feet and is on the same plane as the feet, as the knees are also bent. The hair also flows back horizontally towards the

97

feet. *South Wind* creates the impression of dynamic movement with and through the elements. (See Appendix VI for a listing of Eric's work.)

In 1930 Eric married Winifred Maxfield, a silversmith, and they had one daughter, Jill, born 1933. When they were first married Eric and Freda lived at 84 Charlotte Street, and in 1933 they moved to Parkhill Road in Hampstead.

Eric, with his fine sense of detail, was responsible for many of the scale models made at the studio during the 1920s and 1930s. A small illustrated brochure issued by W. Aumonier and Sons entitled *Architectural Scale Models* emphasized the importance of the scale model in solving outstanding architectural problems in the early stages of construction. For instance, the model of Broadcasting House, Portland Square, London, which Eric made for the architects Val Myers and Watson Hart, was used to solve problems relating to the Fleet River, an underground river that rises in the ponds at Hampstead Heath and flows under Fleet Street before reaching the Thames. Three other models can also be attributed to Eric: an Egyptian estate, the offices of London Electric Railways in Broadway, and the head office of the Westminster Bank in Lothbury. Freda made the lantern, and the silver gates, which were $2^9/_{16}$ inches high, for this last model.[5]

Eric and Freda probably worked together professionally on other occasions, but there is no record of this. Freda taught jewellery design for the London Education Authority, but for the most part she worked privately, designing and making jewellery and small pieces such as coffee spoons. Her designs were modern and attractive.

Eric, Freda, and Jill stayed in London at the beginning of the war in spite of the air raids. Their house was destroyed by a bomb in the early 1940s and Freda and Jill moved to the country. Eric went to live in Wembley Park with Whitworth, Michael, and Elisabeth Anne. After the war Una Cameron, a life-long friend of Freda's, gave her money to buy a house in Radlett. This was an enormous help and slowly Eric and Freda re-established themselves. In addition to his own commissions and work Eric helped out his overworked friends who were having trouble meeting deadlines.

Eric worked in the film industry for several years during and after the war. He worked mostly as a modeller, designing and executing such pieces as statues for the film *Knights of the Round Table*, a sculptured model of Captain Scott for *A Matter of Life and Death*, and statues and stone carvings for *Caesar and Cleopatra*. He worked for several studios, including Denham, Ealing, and Metro-Goldwyn-Mayer, and his position was usually that of assistant to the director.

In the postwar period he designed, carved, and modelled the panels and keystones at the new Bank of England. The centre panel, based on the great seal of 1694, is a stone carving of William and Mary, and at the top of two adjacent stone pillars are statues of the original directors of the bank, the Huguenot Sir John Houblon and Michael Godfrey. In 1957 he designed and carved a panel for the Diamond Corporation of South Africa in Holborn, and in 1959 he designed, modelled, and carved a stone panel for Quaglino's Restaurant in Jermyn Street, depicting Lord St. Jermyn receiving the deeds of Jermyn Street from James I.

In a completely different vein he modelled, cast, and decorated a large piece for the Food Fair at Olympia in 1960, using nursery rhymes as his theme. And in 1951 he produced a piece of modelled sculpture for the Festival of Britain exhibition. Inspired by Tenniel's illustration in *Through the Looking Glass* he made a larger than life-size model of the White Knight. He rented a studio at the Elstree film studios to carry out this work.

Eric was an Associate of the Royal Society of British Sculptors and a member of the Art Workers Guild. He became a member of the Guild in 1950 and was elected to the committee in 1953.

In the early 1960s Eric and Freda emigrated to New Zealand to join Jill, who had moved there some years previously and was now married with children. Eric had never been particularly strong and during the last years of his life he was crippled with rheumatoid arthritis. He died in 1974 with less than the equivalent of £500 in the bank. Jill died in 1982 and Freda in 1995.

‹ ✳ ›

Pierre loved the outdoor life and often said that he should have been born a hundred years earlier and "lived on the frontier of the Canadian Northwest . . .

Eric, Mary, and Dennis, 1928

South Wind, Temple of the Winds, carved by Eric, 1929

Eric working on his stone panel for Quaglino's Restaurant, 1959

Bronze figure by Eric, 1935

Eric working on his nursery-rhyme sculpture for the Food Fair at Olympia, 1960

everything I do seems so natural. I have no fear of getting lost after tramping, twisting, and climbing all day, I instinctively turn in the right direction for camp, without even knowing it!"[6] Pierre was an engineer and by 1931 he was working for the City of Calgary, where he lived. He and his wife Marion adopted two children: Ronald, born 1933, and Joan, born 1935. Marion died in 1941 and in 1943 Pierre married Jessie Addison. They had one daughter, Annette, born 1944. Pierre died in June 1987 and Jessie died in August 1997.

Ronald became a pilot with the Royal Canadian Air Force. He married Patricia Stuart and they have four children, Alexandra, Laurel, Peter, and Gregory.

Annette married Gary Hilton and they have two sons, Michael and Shawn.

‹ * ›

Mary and Dennis were married on 6 July 1929, at St. Cuthbert's Church in Brondesbury, and they lived in Hove in Sussex. They had two daughters: Ann, born 1930, and Julia Mary (Judy), born 1932.

Mary had shown considerable artistic ability from a very early age, and this had been encouraged and fostered by her father, mother, and brothers. After her marriage, however, her interest waned. Maybe she did not receive the encouragement she needed; except for an occasional drawing or sketch, she did not continue with her art.

As a young man Dennis' father had given him a

choice of careers—to become a dentist or a chartered surveyor. He chose the latter and was articled to Graves and Son in Brighton. In 1930 he was made a partner, and the firm was renamed Graves, Son and Pilcher.

During the Second World War Dennis served as an officer in the Royal Artillery. Mary, Ann, and Judy stayed in Hove. There were nightly air-raids and later the flying bombs. For many years they slept in the shelter, which was the cupboard-under-the-stairs reinforced with wooden beams.

After the war Dennis opened a branch of Graves, Son and Pilcher in London. He also worked professionally on a national level, and his many achievements, most notably with new towns, did not go unrecognized: in 1968 he was appointed a Commander of the British Empire and he received a knighthood in 1974.

Mary and Dennis lived in Hove until the late 1960s when they moved to Pulborough. Mary died in September 1991, and Dennis in January 1994.

‹ ✳ ›

The artistic talent in this family lives on. Elisabeth Anne, Whitworth's daughter, is a successful artist. When she was a child she frequently went to the studio with her father on Saturday mornings, and her uncle Eric would set up an easel next to his so that she could draw and paint. Elisabeth paints in both watercolours and oils, and her work is eclectic and experimental. She also designs and creates slides and videos, which are similar in style to her paintings, and she has received the Canada Council Award for some of this work. Her paintings have been exhibited at the Thunder Bay Gallery and the Lakehead Gallery of Visual Arts in Ontario.

Clare, Stacy's granddaughter, is an established sculptor. She lives in Auckland, New Zealand, where she teaches as well as pursuing her own work.

Mary's daughter Judy is a well-established artist. She paints in all media but works principally in acrylics and watercolours. Her paintings are realistic without being photographic and reveal the intensity of her feeling for her subject. She has taught workshops in Italy, Turkey, and England. She exhibits at the Royal Institute of Watercolour Painters, the Federation of British Artists, the Royal West of England Academy, and the New English Art Club. In 1994 she had a successful one-person show in New Delhi: the theme of the exhibition was life in India, and she showed over a hundred watercolour paintings, mostly of women. Judy lives in Winchester with her second husband Tom Strafford. She has three children, Emma, Polly, and Daniel.

Mary's older daughter Ann lives in New City, just outside New York City, with her husband Larry McGill. They were married in 1963 and have two children, Alexandra, born 1964, and Benjamin, born 1966. Alexandra, who is called Lexi, is also an artist: she is a representational expressionist who paints in oils, gouache, acrylic, and mixed media. She studied art at Teachers College (Columbia University), the School of Visual Art in New York, and the Rockland Center for the Arts and has exhibited in New York and Nyack, New York. She currently teaches art in New York City.

‹ * ›

At the end of the twentieth century over three hundred years have passed since Pierre II, a craftsman and an exile, arrived on the shores of England. This account has traced the family through the generations—weavers, jewellers, sculptors, carvers, and artists. Their creations and achievements are part of our heritage.

APPENDICES

‹ ❋ ›

Appendix I

Paintings by James Aumonier (incomplete list)

Where the Water Lilies Grow, exhibited Royal Academy (RA) 1870
Okehampton Castle, Dartmoor, exhibited RA 1871
A Surrey Footbridge, exhibited RA 1872
An English Cottage Home, exhibited RA 1873
An Easter Holyday, exhibited RA 1874
Spring—Peeling Osiers, exhibited RA 1875
Thames at Great Marlow, exhibited RA 1875 & 1876
Toilers of the Field, exhibited RA 1876
Waterlilies, exhibited RA 1876
Easton Broad, Suffolk, exhibited RA 1877
Wheat, near Overton, Hants, exhibited RA 1877
Wasteland, exhibited RA 1878, Guildhall 1897
Whitby Cobbles, exhibited RA 1878
A Suffolk Marsh, exhibited RA 1879, Manchester Jubilee 1887
A Nook in Nature's Garden, exhibited RA 1880, acquired by Birmingham Museum & Art gallery
Oxford, exhibited RA 1880
London, from Greenwich Park, exhibited RA 1881
Homeward, exhibited RA 1884
The Way through the Wood, exhibited RA 1884
A Village Green, exhibited RA 1885

June, "When the long drooping boughs, . . ." exhibited
RA 1886

The Village Congregation, exhibited RA 1886

The Close of Day (mezzotint), exhibited RA 1886

The Last Load, exhibited Manchester Jubilee 1887

In Fold, exhibited RA 1887

Football, exhibited RA 1888

Sussex Gold, exhibited RA 1888

Carrying the Wheat, exhibited RA 1889

Sheep Washing, purchased by Tate Gallery, Chantrey Bequest 1889, exhibited RA 1899

A Mill by the Sea, exhibited RA 1890

The Silver Lining of the Cloud, exhibited RA 1890,
acquired by City of Manchester 1890

Sunday Evening, exhibited RA 1891

The River Piave, Belluno, Venetia, exhibited RA
1892

Belluno, Venetia, exhibited RA 1893

Lancing Mill, Sussex, exhibited RA 1893, acquired
for Tasmania 1893

On the South Downs, exhibited RA 1894

In the Valley of the Arun, exhibited RA 1895

When the Tide is Out, exhibited RA 1895

The Old Sussex Farmhouse, exhibited Royal Institute
(RI) 1895

In the Fen Country, exhibited RA 1896

Old Chalk Pit, exhibited RI 1896

A Hayfield, exhibited RA 1897

Grazing Land, exhibited RA 1897

A Wide Pasture, exhibited RA 1898

An Autumn Afternoon, exhibited RA 1900

A Lonely Heath, exhibited RA 1901

A Herefordshire Common, exhibited RA 1903, acquired for Melbourne 1903

The Borderlands, exhibited RA 1904

Black Mountains, exhibited RA 1905, purchased
   by Tate Gallery, Chantrey Bequest 1905

Chantrey Work, exhibited RA 1905

The Top of the Common, exhibited RA 1906

Dulas Valley, exhibited RA 1907

Evening on the Downs, shown Goupil Gallery 1907

A Spanish Village, painted 1908

Amersham Common, exhibited RA 1908

Evening, Franco-British exhibition 1908

On a Fen Farm, Franco-British exhibition 1908,
   British Empire Exhibition 1924

The School Feast, Franco-British exhibition 1908

Under the Beech Trees, exhibited Old Water Colour
   Society Gallery 1908

Castle Valley, Tintagel, exhibited RA 1909, Japan
   exhibition, 1910

"The day's work is done," exhibited RA 1910

On the Barrow Downs, Dorset, exhibited RA 1911

A Common (1903)

An Upland Meadow

At Gilsand, Northumberland

At Wrangle, Lincolnshire

Cold Windy Day, acquired by Leeds

Coombe Lane, Lancing, Sussex

East Ashling, Sussex

Elms in Spring Time, East Ashling, Sussex

Evening on the Southdowns

Evening Sunlight

Farm Horses Drinking at a Pond

Flock of Sheep, near Maldon, Essex

Gathering Bait, acquired by Walker Gallery, Liverpool

Harting near Lancing, Sussex
Harvest Moon
Harvesters
Haymaking
Horses Drinking at a Pond
Lonely Valley, Evening
Market Day
Noon on the Downs, near Shoreham
Nr. Maldon, Essex
Old Shoreham, acquired by Capetown
Sand Barges, Shoreham, Sussex
Scottish Moor
Sheep on the Downs
Ship by a Stream
Southwold, Suffolk
Spring
Sunset on the Sussex Downs, acquired by Birming-
    ham Museum and Art Gallery
Sussex Hay Field
Three sketches, acquired by Cardiff
View of Lancing College
Village Smithy
Wild Flowers

‹ ❊ ›

Appendix II

Paintings by Jack (John) Aumonier exhibited
at the Royal Academy

Carricks Road, exhibited 1903
The Coastguard Station, exhibited 1906
April in the Somme Valley, exhibited 1921
Le Printemps, exhibited 1921
The Country of the Severn and the Wye, exhibited 1925
Painswick Mill, exhibited 1929
St. Généri-sur-Sarthe (tempera), exhibited 1930

‹ ❉ ›

Appendix III

Carving, modelling, and sculpture by William Aumonier, Sr. (incomplete list)

Avery Hill College, Bexley Hill, Eltham: wood carving; architect, T. W. Cutler (1891)

Bath Art Gallery: capitals; architect, J. M. Brydon

Birmingham Law Courts, gable modelled in terra cotta; architects, Aston Webb & Ingress (1889); design for gable exhibited at Royal Academy 1899

Debenham House: wood carving, timber staircase; architect, Halsey Ricardo

London School Board office, Victoria Embankment; architects, Bodley and Garner

St. Paul's Cathedral, London: the pediment and back of the Bishop's Throne, Sedilla and Fald stool; architects, Bodley and Garner

Town Hall and Library, Katherine Street, Croydon, armorial carving; architect, Charles Henner Jr. (1892–6)

Wordsworth Buildings, Lady Margaret Hall, Oxford, wood carving; architect, Sir Reginald Blomfield (1897)

‹ ❋ ›

Appendix IV

Titles of books written by Stacy Aumonier

Olga Bardel, 1916
The Friends, and Other Stories, 1917
Just Outside, 1917
Three Bars' Interval, 1917
The Querrils, 1919
One After Another, 1920
Golden Windmill and Other Stories, 1921
The Love-a-Duck and Other Stories, 1921
Heartbeat, 1922
Miss Bracegirdle and Others, 1923
Overheard: Fifteen Tales, 1924
The Baby Grand and Other Stories, 1926
Selected Essays, 1926
Ups and Downs: A Collection of Stories, 1929
Little Windows, 1931

Odd Fish, with George Belcher, 1923

⟨ ✻ ⟩

Appendix V

Carving, modelling, and sculpture by William
Aumonier, Jr. (incomplete list)

Alfreton War Memorial, stone carving

Anglo-Egyptian Bank, King William Street, stone carving; architect, W. Campbell Jones, Son and Smithers

Australia House, the Aldwych, stone carving; architect, Marshall Mackenzie (1912–18)

Baring's Bank, Bishopsgate, carving at entrance; architect, Gerald Horsely

Berrington Hall, Herefordshire, war memorial to three sons of Lord and Lady Cawley; architect, Sir Reginald Blomfield

British Medical Association, Strand, carved wood panels; architects, Percy Adams and Charles Holden (completed 1929)

Burford Church, Oxon., triptych; architect, Sir Aston Webb

Carlton Club, Pall Mall, stone carving; architect, Sir Reginald Blomfield

Gas Light & Coke Company, Church Street, keyblocks; architects, Whinney, Son & Austen Hall (1926)

Henley Town Hall, interior carving; architect, H. T. Hare

Hong Kong & Shanghai Bank, Moorgate, stone carving, marble clock case; architects, W. Campbell Jones, Son and Smithers (1914–1920)

Hoppers' Memorial, Paddock Wood, stone relief; from design by Gordon Hake

Knowsley Hall, Prescot, Merseyside, coat of arms for Lord Derby, stone carving; architect, W. H. Romaine-Walker

Leathersellers Company, St. Helen's Place, coat of arms, stone carving; architects, Mewes and Davis (1928)

Lloyds Bank, near King William Street, stone carving; architects, W. Campbell Jones, Son and Smithers

London Assurance company, near King William Street, stone carving; architects, W. Campbell Jones, Son and Smithers

Menin Gate, Ypres; architect, Sir Reginald Blomfield

Merchant Marine Insurance Company, near King William Street, stone carving; architect, W. Campbell Jones, Son and Smithers

Merchant Taylors Hall, Threadneedle Street, heraldic carving and cartouche to chimney piece

Midland Bank, Piccadilly, wood carving; architects, Whinney, Son & Austen Hall

Midland Bank, Southampton, stone carving; architects, Whinney, Son & Austen Hall

North Eastern Railway Company, Cowley Place, Westminster, woodcarving in board room; architect, Horace Field

Prince of Wales statue, Bombay, cartouche and bronze coat of arms

Provident Mutual Assurance, Moorgate, stone carving at entrance; architects, W. Campbell Jones, Son and Smithers (1922)

Regent Street, quadrant end and Criterion corner, stone carving; architect, Sir Reginald Blomfield (1920–23)

Somerville College, Oxford, wood carving, memorial panelling; architect, E. Fisher

St. Luke's Church, Redcliffe Square, wood carving, organ case; architects, the Godwins (1920)

Tenison Memorial, Cloisters Canterbury Cathedral; from design by Gordon Hake

Westminster Bank, Threadneedle Street, stone carving; architects, Mewes and Davis

Trinity College of Music, stone front (exterior), and figure of Pan carved in oak for the overdoor (interior); architect, J. O. Cheadle

Usher Gallery, Lincoln; architect, Sir Reginald Blomfield

Wandsworth Trust, Long Sutton, gateway; architect, Sir Reginald Blomfield

Westminster Bank, Angel Court, Lothbury, stone carving; architect, Mewes and Davis

⟨ ❋ ⟩

Appendix VI

Carving, modelling, and sculpture by Eric Aumonier
(incomplete list)

Bank of England, New Change, panels: William and Mary, *Midas* and *Bacchus,* architect, Victor Heal

Bank of South America, London, roundels designed, modelled, and painted by Eric for Esmond Burton; architect, Victor Heal (1958)

Barber Institute, Birmingham, carved panels depicting musical instruments; architect, Robert Atkinson

Biddle's bookshop, Guildford, shop sign designed and carved by Eric; commissioned by Rowley

British Broadcasting Corporation, Portland Place, coat of arms; architect, Val Myers and Watson Hart (1931)

Cinéma de Paris, London; two cement figures, *Comedy* and *Tragedy;* architect, Robert Atkinson

Dagenham Town Hall, carvings: *Minerva, Neptune,* and *Villan* (1936)

Daily Express, Fleet Street, main entrance, panels modelled in clay, cast in plaster, and covered in gold leaf: *The Empire* and *Great Britain;* architect, Robert Atkinson (1932)

Diamond Corporation of South Africa, Holborn, clock panel, designed and carved by Eric; architect, Sir Thomas Bennett (1957)

Divinity, Oxford, gothic pinnacle

East Finchley Station, *The Archer* (1940)

East Sheen Cinema, terra cotta panels; architects, Leather and Granger

Festival of Britain, The Lion and the Unicorn Pavilion on the South Bank, *The White Knight* (1951)

Headquarters of the London Underground, St. James's Park Station, *The South Wind* (1929)

Leicester Square Theatre, *Blackmoor* (1952)

Margate Cinema, figures of Pan and panels of fish

New York World's Fair, 1939, Royal Arms; architect, Easton and Robertson

Norwich Town Hall, stone carving of Angel, designed by Eric

Olympia Food Fair, model of nursery-rhyme characters

Quaglino's Restaurant, Jermyn Street, for Esmond Burton, stone panel designed, modelled, and carved by E. A. Theme: *Lord St. Jermyn receiving deeds of Jermyn Street from James I;* architect Victor Neal (1957)

NOTES

‹ ❋ ›

Notes

‹ I ›

Pierre I, Pierre II, and Jonas

1. J. C. Aumonier, "Aumonier, A Huguenot Family," *Proceedings of the Huguenot Society of London* (hereafter *HSP*), vol. XVIII, no. 4, p. 315.

2. R. Gwynn, *Huguenot Heritage*, p. 91.

3. Ibid., p. 93.

4. Ibid., pp. 71, 101, 124.

5. Ibid., p. 108.

6. "Memories of Spitalfields," *HSP*, vol. XXI, pp. 330–1.

7. Gwynn, *Huguenot Heritage*, p. 67.

8. *HSP*, vol. XXVII, pp. 87, 90.

9. *HSP*, vol. XXXIII, p. 73. The Weavers Guild had been granted a Royal Charter in 1130.

10. *HSP*, vol. XII, introduction, p. xviii. Pierre's apprentices included: James Magneron (1719); Peter Bourneau (1724); Lewis Tesir (1725); and Alexander Thorould. (*HSP*, vol. XXXIII, pp. 82, 92–3, 96.)

11. *HSP*, vol. XI, pp. 33, 50.

12. C. Hibbert, *The English: A Social History 1066–1945*, p. 335.

13. R. Gwynn, "The Distribution of Huguenot Refugees in England, II: London and its Environs," *HSP*, vol. XXII, p. 537.

14. *HSP*, vol. V, p. 531.

15. *HSP*, vol. XV, p. 209.

16. *HSP*, vol. XI, p. 78.

17. *HSP*, vol. XII, p. 192.

‹ II ›

Mid Eighteenth Century: Pierre III and David

1. P. Thornton and N. Rothstein, "Huguenots in the English Silk Industry in the Eighteenth Century," *Proceedings of the Huguenot Society of London*, vol. XX; I. Scouloudi, *Huguenots in Britain and their French Background*, p. 126.

2. *HSP*, vol. XI, p. 192.

3. The Statute of Apprentices, passed in 1563 during the reign of Elizabeth I, regulated the terms and conditions of an apprenticeship.

4. Peter Goley and Marie Aumônier were married at St. Anne's Church, Soho, on 17 September 1752. They had three children: Pierre, born 1753; Marie, born 1754; and Jean, born 1756.

5. J. Swann, *Shoes*, pp. 27, 30, 24.

6. Aumonier, "A Huguenot Family," p. 316.

7. *HSP*, vol. XII, p. 153; *HSP*, vol. XXI, p. 8.

8. *HSP*, vol. XVIII, no. 4, p. 316.

9. A maker of paper hangings.

10. John Fleming and Hugh Honour, *The Penguin Dictionary of Decorative Arts*.

‹ III ›

John and Mary: A Love Match

1. The Guild of the London Goldsmiths was incorporated by Royal Charter in 1327 under the title "The Wardens

and Commonalty of the Mystery of Goldsmiths in the City of London." The Goldsmiths' Hall was built in 1340 and has been rebuilt four times on its original site on Foster Lane. Hallmarks: the Leopard's Head, established in 1300, became in 1363 the King's Mark and signified that the object had been tested and found to be of the required standard of purity; the Maker Mark was impressed on the piece after it had been assayed; the Date Letter, which was first known as the "Hall Mark," indicated the year the piece was tested; the Lion Passant was adopted as the official stamp at Goldsmiths Hall in London in 1544. (J. M. Dennis, *English Silver*, pp. 13–15; S. Wyler, *Old Silver*, pp. 8, 12.)

2. John to Mary Everard, 30 March 1793.

3. Ibid., 7 July 1793.

4. Marie L'Homme (née Bourdon) gave birth to a daughter, Elizabeth, in December 1793. There were three other children, Marie, born 1792, Jacques, born 1795, and Louise, born 1798. (*International Genealogical Index*, A1397.)

5. John to Mary Everard, March 30 and May 22, 1793.

6. Ibid., 22 May 1793.

7. *HSP*, vol. XXXIX, p. 79.

‹ IV ›

The Jewellers: Henry, Frederic, and David

1. Registers of makers' marks, Goldsmiths' Hall, London.

2. J. Culme, *Directory of Goldsmiths & Silversmiths 1838–1914*, vol. II, p. 91.

3. The grave was fourteen feet deep. It cost £4 9s for seven feet, plus an additional 16s for "Extra Depth of Grave to 14 feet." The headstone cost 12 guineas with an additional charge of 15s 6d for the inscription of ninety letters.

4. Culme, *Goldsmiths & Silversmiths,* pp. 20, 21.

5. Family papers.

6. John Greswell's mark was IG, entered at Goldsmiths' Hall on 12 April 1824. (Registers of makers' marks, Goldsmiths' Hall.)

7. Goldsmiths' Hall records.

8. *The British Library Catalogue,* 1991.

9. E. A. Entwistle, *Wallpaper of the Victorian Era,* p. 37.

10. Fleming and Honour, *Decorative Art.*

11. Advertisement for William Woollams and Co. (about 1900).

12. *The Royal Academy of Arts Exhibits 1769–1904;* E. Bénézit, *Dictionnaire critique et documentaire des peintres, sculpteurs, dessinateurs et graveurs* (1976); C. Petteys, *Dictionary of Women Artists.*

‹ V ›

James

1. N. Bell, "James Aumonier and His Work," *The International Studio* (1900), vol. XI, p. 141.

2. The Institute was founded in 1823 by Dr. Birkbeck and was later renamed Birkbeck College. (N. Pevsner, Walter Neurath memorial lectures, 1969, p. 43.)

3. *Dictionary of National Biography* (supplement).

4. Bell, "James Aumonier," pp. 141, 142.

5. W. Bayes, "The Landscape Paintings of James Aumonier," *The International Studio* (1910), vol. XXXIX, p. 175.

6. Ibid., pp. 183, 185.

7. *Royal Academy of Art Exhibitors 1769 to 1904,* p. 79.

8. Bayes, "Paintings of James Aumonier," p. 175.

9. In 1848 the school moved from Maddox Street to 79

Newman Street with James Matthew Leigh as Principal. Thomas Heatherley was Principal from 1860 to 1887. In 1907 it moved to 75 Newman Street and in 1927 to George Street. It was closed during the Second World War. After the war, in 1946, it was amalgamated with the Grosvenor School of Modern Art and re-opened at Warwick Square, where it remained until 1977.

10. Bell, "James Aumonier," p. 142.

11. Bayes, "Paintings of James Aumonier," p. 180; *Dictionary of National Biography*, p. 71.

12. Bénézit, *Dictionnaire;* City of Birmingham Museum and Art Gallery, *Illustrated Catalogue of the Permanent Collection of Paintings, 1899.*

13. The Royal Institute was founded in 1832 as the New Watercolour Society and became the Institute of Painters in Watercolours in 1863. It became the Royal Institute of Painters in Watercolours at a later date.

14. The Old Watercolour Society's Galleries had been founded in 1804 by a Dr. Monroe and a group of watercolourists as an alternative to the Royal Academy for showing their work. It received a royal charter in 1881.

15. Dictionary of National Biography (supplement), p. 71; A. Graves, *A Century of Loan Exhibitions 1813–1912;* Bénézit, *Dictionnaire;* Birmingham Museum and Art Gallery, *Illustrated Catalogue.*

16. H. Rodee, "Background for Scenes of Rural Poverty in Victorian Painting," *The Art Journal* (1977), p. 312.

17. Tate Gallery, *Catalogue of the British School,* 25th edition; Birmingham Museum and Art Gallery, *Illustrated Catalogue.*

18. Bell, "James Aumonier," p. 146; *Dictionary of Victorian Painters,* 2nd edition. The New English Art Club was founded in 1886 by a group of young artists. The artists, not a commit-

tee, selected the pictures to be shown—this was the custom in French art societies at that time.

19. Sydney Parvière, *A Dictionary of Victorian Landscape Painters*.

20. Family papers.

21. K. L. Mallalieu, *Dictionary of British Watercolour Artists up to 1920*; Official Guide of the British Empire Exhibition, 1924.

22. *Royal Academy Exhibitions 1905 to 1970*.

‹ VI ›

William and the Aumonier Studio

1. Dennis Farr, *English Art 1870 to 1940*, p. 21.

2. Possibly Charles Kaltenheuser, sculptor, born in Barmen (now part of Wuppertal), Germany, and Pierre Fourdrinier, wood engraver, born in France. (Bénézit, *Dictionnaire*.)

3. Bénézit, *Dictionnaire*; Macmillan Encyclopedia of Architects.

4. Highgate cemetery, grave 155.

5. *The Builder*, 21 December 1889; *Royal Academy of Art Exhibitions 1769–1904*. William exhibited a drawing, *Symbolic Figures*, at the Royal Academy in 1890.

6. W. Aumonier, "Veneer Work and Solid Inlay," *Journal of the Royal Society of British Architects*, Third Series, vol. IX (1902), no. 11, pp. 288, 290.

7. *The Builder*, 1897. E. Jones and Christopher Woodward, *A Guide to the Architecture of London*, p. 160; Aumonier, "A Huguenot Family," p. 319. Restoration of Chequers began in 1909 when Lord and Lady Lee entered into a long tenancy. In 1917 they changed their tenancy into a freehold and established a trust which, upon their death, would make

the house and estate an adequate country seat for prime ministers. In 1920, however, they decided that this should not wait until their death, and Lloyd George began to use the house the following year.

8. Aymer Vallance, "British Decorative Art in 1899 and the Arts and Crafts Exhibition," *International Studio,* vol. IX (1900), p. 265.

9. (1) 3 February 1896: *Wood-Carving and Wood-Carvers*; fellow speakers, W. H. Romaine-Walker, J. E. Knox and W. S. Frith. (2) 7 April 1902: *Inlay and Marquetry* (William's paper was entitled *Veneer Work and Solid Inlay*); fellow speaker, Heywood Sumner. (3) 9 April 1906: *Wood-carving*; fellow speaker, A. W. Martyn.

10. W. Aumonier, "Wood-Carving and Wood-Carvers," *Journal of the Royal Society of British Architects,* Third Series, vol. III (1896), no. 7, p. 211.

11. W. Aumonier, "Woodcarving," *Journal of the Royal Society of British Architects,* Third Series, vol. XIII (1906), no. 11, p. 291.

12. H. J. L. J. Massé, *The Art Workers Guild 1884 to 1934,* p. 136; Dennis Farr, *English Art 1870–1940,* p. 137.

13. Massé, *Art Workers Guild,* p. 76.

14. Ibid., *Art Workers Guild,* p. 87.

15. *Royal Academy Exhibitions 1905–1970.*

‹ VII ›

Stacy

1. Cranleigh School records. William and James, Stacy's father and uncle, were both well known in London at that time.

2. *Royal Academy Exhibitions 1905 to 1970.*

3. Kunitz and Haycraft, *Twentieth Century Authors; The Times* (London), December 1929 (Stacy's obituary).

4. *The Royal Academy of Art Exhibitors 1769 to 1904,* vol. I; Kunitz and Haycraft, *Twentieth Century Authors;* Mallalieu, *British Watercolour Artists.*

5. Kunitz and Haycraft, *Twentieth Century Authors.*

6. Kunitz and Haycraft, *Twentieth Century Authors*; John Galsworthy, foreword to *Ups and Downs,* by Stacy Aumonier; *The Times* (London), December 1929.

7. Kunitz and Haycraft, *Twentieth Century Authors.*

8. Stacy to John Galsworthy, Dorset, 3 September 1926. (Harold V. Marrot, *The Life and Letters of John Galsworthy,* pp. 578, 579.)

9. Rebecca West papers, The Beinecke Rare Book and Manuscript Library, Yale University.

10. Letters from Julia Aumonier to Pierre Aumonier, 9 October, 14 November, 1927.

11. Rebecca West papers, The Beinecke Rare Book and Manuscript Library.

12. *The Times* (London), 11 June 1929.

‹ VIII ›

84 Charlotte Street

1. Julia Augusta's mother, Wynanda Sophia, was married twice. Her first husband was Joseph Gutierrez and they had three children: Wynanda, John, and Henry Lumley James. Her second husband was Julia Augusta's father, Captain Michael Whitworth. Julia Augusta was their only child.

2. Kineton Parkes, "Modern English Carvers, The Aumonier family," *The Architectural Review,* Nov. 1927, vol. II, pp. 192–3.

3. W. H. Manchee, *Huguenot London, HSP*, vol. XIII, no. 1, p. 68 (read before the Huguenot Society, Nov. 1923).

4. W. Aumonier, "More Thoughts on Stone Carving," *The Architectural Review,* April 1926, vol. XXIX, p. 11.

5. Parkes, "Modern English Carvers," pp. 192–3.

6. Article, *Alfreton and Belper Journal.*

7. Official Guide of the British Empire Exhibition, 1924, p. 97. The amusement park extended over fifty acres and was described as one of the largest pleasure parks on record.

8. Article, *St. Pancras Chronicle,* 29 June 1928.

9. Massé, *Art Workers Guild,* p. 136.

10. Memberships and affiliations: The Art Workers Guild, The Architectural Association, The Architecture Club, Master Carvers Association, The Arts Lodge (Masonic), The Arts and Crafts Lodge (Masonic), The Studio Club, The Arts Club (Dover Street), The St. John's Wood Art Club, and United University Club.

11. Pasteur D. Bourchenin to Willie, 8 March 1927.

‹ IX ›

Family Life: Willie and Julia

1. Julia to her son Pierre, 16 February 1928.
2. Ibid.
3. Ibid., 12 May 1926.
4. Ibid., 2 October 1927.
5. Ibid., 9 October 1927.
6. Ibid., 30 May 1926.
7. Ibid., 11 May 1926.
8. Ibid., 30 May, 14 June 1926.
9. Ibid., 26 February 1928.
10. Ibid., 14, 28 November 1927.

11. Ibid., 26 February 1928.
12. Ibid., 16 February, 21 July 1928.
13. Ibid., 21 July 1928.
14. Willie to Pierre, 4 October 1928.
15. Article, Montreal newspaper, August 1930.
16. Article, *The World*, New York, 15 November 1930.
17. Article, *Leeds Mercury*, 17 March 1933.
18. Newspaper article, March 1933.
19. Willie to Pierre, 26 August 1940.

‹ X ›

Whitworth, Eric, Pierre, and Mary

1. Parkes, "Modern English Carvers," p. 192.
2. Massé, *Art Workers Guild*, p. 136.
3. Eric Aumonier—*South Wind* on the west side of the north wing; Allan Wyon—*East Wind* on the south side of the west wing; Eric Gill—*South Wind* on the east side of the north wing, *North Wind* on the east side of the south wing, *East Wind* on the north side of the west wing; A. H. Gerard—*North Wind* on the west side of the south wing; F. Rabinovitch—*West Wind* on the south side of the east wing; and Henry Moore—*West Wind* on the north side of the east wing.
4. Kineton Parkes, *Art of Carved Sculpture*, vol. I, p. 80.
5. Family papers.
6. Pierre to Whitworth, September 1933.

BIBLIOGRAPHY

< ❊ >

Bibliography

Aumonier, J. C. "Aumônier: A Huguenot Family from Haut-Poitou." *Proceedings of the Huguenot Society of London,* vol. XVIII, no. 4.

Aumonier, William. "Wood Carving and Wood Carvers." *Journal of the Royal Institute of British Architects,* third series, vol. III (1896).

Aumonier, William. "Veneer Work and Solid Inlay." *Journal of the Royal Institute of British Architects,* third series, vol. IX (1902).

Aumonier, William. "Wood-carving." *Journal of the Royal Institute of British Architects,* third series, vol. XIII (1906).

Aumonier, William, ed. *Modern Architectural Sculpture.* London: Architectural Press, Charles Scribner's Sons, 1930.

Bannister, Judith. *English Silver.* New York: Paul Hamlyn, 1969.

Barnhart, Clarence, ed. *New Century Handbook of English Literature.* New York: Appleton-Century-Crofts, 1956.

———, ed. *New Century Cyclopædia of Names.* New York: Appleton-Century-Crofts, 1954.

Bayes, Walter. "The Landscape Painting of James Aumonier." *International Studio,* vol. XXXIX (1910).

Beattie, Susan. *The New Sculpture.* New Haven and London: Yale University Press, 1983.

Bell, Nancy. "James Aumonier and His Work." *International Studio,* vol. XI (1900).

Bénézit, G. *Dictionnaire critique et documentaire des peintres, sculp-*

teurs, dessinateurs et graveurs de tous les temps et de tous les pays. Paris: Grund, 1976.

Boeck, Urs. *Sculpture on Building.* New York: Universe Books, 1961.

Briggs, Asa. *A Social History of England.* London: Viking Press, 1984.

The British Empire Exhibition, 1924. *Official Guide.* London: Fleetway Press, 1924.

———. *Illustrated Souvenir of the Palace of Arts, 1925.*

The Builder. 13 February 1897.

City of Birmingham Museum and Art Gallery: *Illustrated Catalogue of the Permanent Collection of Paintings,* 1899.

Clapp, Jane. *Sculpture Index.* Metuchen, New Jersey: Scarecrow Press, 1970–71

Cook, Dorothy E., and Monroe, Isabel. *Short Story Index.* New York: H. W. Wilson Co., 1953.

Culme, John. *The Directory of Gold and Silversmiths; Jewellers and Allied Traders 1838–1914: from the London Assay Office Registers.* Woodbridge, Suffolk: Antique Collectors Club, 1987.

Curtis, Penelope, ed. *Patronage and Practice: Sculpture on Merseyside.* Liverpool: Tate Gallery and National Gallery & Museums on Merseyside, 1989.

Darke, Jo. *The Monument Guide to England and Wales.* London: MacDonald, 1991.

Dennis, Jessie McNab. *English Silver.* New York: Walker & Co., 1970.

Dictionary of National Biography. Oxford: Oxford University Press, 1970.

Duthoit, Aimé et Louis. *En Picardie et alentours. Dessiné d'après nature.* Picardie, CRDP, 1979

Entwistle, E. A. *Wallpapers of the Victorian Era.* Leigh-on-Sea: F. Lewis, 1964.

Evans, Joan. *A History of Jewellery. 1110–1870.* Dover, 1989.

Farr, Dennis. *English Art 1870–1940.* Oxford: Oxford University Press, 1978.

Fisher, Stanley. *A Dictionary of Watercolour Painters 1750–1900.* London: W. Foulton, 1972.

Fleming, John, and Honour, Hugh. *The Penguin Dictionary of Decorative Arts,* rev. ed. New York: Viking Penguin, 1989.

Flower, Margaret. *Victorian Jewellery.* New York: Duell, Sloan & Pearce, 1951.

Galsworthy, John. Foreword to *Ups and Downs.* London: William Heinemann, 1929.

Graves, Algernon. *A Century of Loan Exhibitions 1813–1912.* New York: Burt Franklin, 1913.

Gwynn, Robin D. *Huguenot Heritage.* London and Boston: Routledge & Kegan Paul, 1985.

————. "The Distribution of Huguenot Refugees in England, II: London and its Environs." *Proceedings of the Huguenot Society of London,* vol. XXII.

Hart, Roger. *English Life in the Seventeenth Century.* New York: G. P. Putnam's Sons, 1970.

————. *English Life in the Eighteenth Century.* New York: G. P. Putnam's Sons, 1970.

————. *English Life in the Nineteenth Century.* New York: G. P. Putnam's Sons, 1971.

Hibbert, Christopher. *The English. A Social History 1066–1945.* London: W. H. Norton & Sons, 1987.

Hoving, Thomas. *Tutankhamun—The Untold Story:* New York: Simon & Schuster, 1978.

Huguenot Society of London Quarto Series Publications.

James, T. G. H. *Howard Carter: The Path to Tutankhamun.* London and New York: Kegan Paul International, 1992.

Jones, Edward, and Woodward, Christopher, eds. *A Guide to the Architecture of London.* London: Thames & Hudson, 1982.

Kitchen, G. W. *A History of France,* vols. II & III. Oxford: Clarendon Press, 1877.

Kunitz, S. J., and Haycraft, H., eds. *Twentieth Century Authors.* New York: H. W. Wilson, 1942.

Kuntzsch, Ingrid. *A History of Jewels and Jewellery.* New York: St. Martin's Press, 1981.

Mallalieu, K. L. *Dictionary of British Watercolour Artists up to 1920.* London: Antique Collectors Club, 1976.

Marrot, Harold Vincent. *The Life and Letters of John Galsworthy.* New York: Charles Scribner's Sons, 1936.

Martin, Rev. J. A. *Christian Firmness of the Huguenots and Sketch of the History of the French Refugee Church of Canterbury.* London: S. W. Partridge & Co., 1881.

Massé, Henri Jean Louis Joseph. *The Art Workers Guild, 1884–1934.* Oxford: Shakespeare Head Press, 1935.

Nairne, Sandy, and Serota, Nicholas, eds. *British Sculpture in the Twentieth Century.* London: Whitechapel Art Gallery, 1981.

Parkes, Kineton. *Art of Carved Sculpture, Vol. I: Western Europe.* London: Chapman & Hall, 1931.

————. "Modern English Carvers, The Aumonier Family." *The Architectural Review,* Nov. 1927, vol. II.

Parvière, Sydney. *A Dictionary of Victorian Landscape Painters.* Leigh-on-Sea: F. Lewis, 1968.

Pevsner, Nikolaus, revised by Bridget Cherry. *The Buildings of England.* Harmondsworth, Middlesex: Penguin, 1973.

Pevsner, Nikolaus. *Ruskin and Viollet-Le-Duc: Englishness and Frenchness in the Appreciation of Gothic Art.* Walter Neurath Memorial Lectures, 1969. London: Thames & Hudson, 1969.

Placzek, K., ed. *Macmillan Encyclopædia of Architects:* New York: Free Press; London: Collier Macmillan, 1982.

Plummer, Alfred. *The London Weavers' Company.* London and Boston: Routledge & Kegan Paul, 1972.

Pooley, Sir Ernest. *The Guilds of the City of London.* London: Collins, 1958

BIBLIOGRAPHY

Proceedings of the Huguenot Society of London.

Quennell, Marjorie. *A History of Everyday Things in England, Vol. IV, 1851–1914.* New York: Putnam, 1958.

Rodee, Howard D. "The 'Dreary Landscape' as Grounds for Scenes of Rural Victorian Paintings." *Art Journal,* vol. XXXVI, no. 4 (1977).

The Royal Academy of Arts Exhibitors 1769–1904. London: SRP & Langmead, 1970.

Royal Academy Exhibitions 1905–1970. Yorkshire: EP Publishing Ltd., 1978.

Scarisbrick, Diane. *Jewellery.* London: F. T. Batsford, 1984.

Scouloudi, Irene, ed. *Huguenots in Britain and Their French Background, 1550–1800: Contributions to the Historical Conference of the Huguenot Society of London, 24–25 September 1985.* Basingstoke, Hants: Macmillan, c1987.

Steinbrunner, C., Penzler, O., Lachman, M., and Shibuk, C., eds. *Encyclopædia of Mystery and Detection.* New York: McGraw-Hill Book Co., 1976.

Swann, June. *Shoes.* London: F. T. Batsford, 1982.

Tate Gallery. *Catalogue of British School,* 25th ed. 1947.

Thornton, Peter, and Rothstein, Natalie. "The Importance of the Huguenots in the London Silk Industry." *Proceedings of the Huguenot Society of London,* vol. XX.

Vallance, Aymer. "British Decorative Art in 1899 and the Arts and Crafts Exhibition, Part IV." *International Studio,* vol. IX (1900).

Warren, Edward. "Obituary of William Aumonier." *The Architectural Review,* vol. XXXV (1914).

Wood, Christopher. *Dictionary of Victorian Painters,* 2nd ed. London: Antique Collectors Club, 1978.

Wyler, Seymour B. *The Book of Old Silver.* New York: Crown Publishers, 1937.

Young, Elizabeth and Wayland. *Old London Churches.* London: Faber & Faber, 1956.

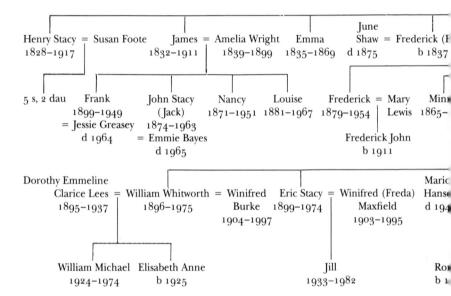

(John) Henry Collingwood Aumonier
1799–1848

Henry Stacy = Susan Foote   James = Amelia Wright   Emma   June Shaw = Frederick (F
1828–1917   1832–1911   1839–1899   1835–1869   d 1875   b 1837

5 s, 2 dau   Frank   John Stacy   Nancy   Louise   Frederick = Mary   Min
              1899–1949   (Jack)   1871–1951   1881–1967   1879–1954 Lewis   1865–
              = Jessie Greasey 1874–1963
              d 1964   = Emmie Bayes   Frederick John
                            d 1965   b 1911

Dorothy Emmeline   Maric
Clarice Lees = William Whitworth = Winifred   Eric Stacy = Winifred (Freda)   Hanse
1895–1937   1896–1975   Burke   1899–1974   Maxfield   d 194
                                  1904–1997   1903–1995

        William Michael Elisabeth Anne   Jill   Ror
        1924–1974   b 1925   1933–1982   b 1